Commonwealth
and Community
The Jewish Experience in Virginia

Melvin I. Urofsky

Virginia Historical Society

and

Jewish Community Federation of Richmond

Richmond 1997

ISBN 0-945015-16-X

Printed in the United States of America

Composition by Cadmus Journal Services, Richmond, Virginia
Printed by Cadmus Promotional Print Division, Sandston, Virginia
Photography by Ronald H. Jennings
Cover design by Melissa J. Savage

Cover: Lewis and Rosalie Hutzler Held with their children, Amelia, Fanny, Mathilda, and Isaac, photographed in Richmond about 1857 *(Beth Ahabah Museum and Archives)*

Back: Death certificate of Rebecca Frank Mirmelstein of Newport News *(courtesy of Rita Spirn)*

Generous funding from S. Sidney and Anne H. Meyers, the Honorable Ezra and Katherine Meyers Cohen, and Michael and Nancy Meyers Marsiglia in memory of Naomi S. Cohn and Selma Cohn Meyers supported the publication of this work.

Contents

ACKNOWLEDGMENTS

"COMMONWEALTH and Community: The Jewish Experience in Virginia" is an exhibition in which we show both the unique aspects of the Jewish experience and how it fits into the larger tapestry of the story of Virginia. In that respect, this has been an important project for the Virginia Historical Society in partnership with the Jewish Community Federation of Richmond. Although the historical society has done a good job of interpreting the history of most Virginians, it has not examined in depth the experience of Virginia Jews. This exhibition has given us that opportunity. It has entailed a thorough evaluation of the latest scholarship, as well as substantial original research.

The people who have worked on this project are numerous, but two people stand out as key architects. Saul Viener, a former trustee of the historical society and a recognized authority on southern Judaism, approached me some two years ago about the possibility of an exhibition on the Jewish experience in Virginia. His enthusiasm was contagious, and I am delighted we could act on his recommendation. Since then, Saul has been an invaluable member of the team and provided copious research. Just as important, however, have been his fund-raising talents. Again using his skills of persuasion, he was able to raise more than $50,000 for this project. Also, early in the planning process, Melvin I. Urofsky, a trustee of the historical society and professor of history at Virginia Commonwealth University, joined the project as guest historian. Award-winning author of several books, including a biography of Justice Louis Brandeis, Dr. Urofsky brought a depth and breadth of knowledge that was invaluable. Thanks in no small part to the efforts of Saul Viener and Mel Urofsky, this project has been a success.

There have been other crucial players. James C. Kelly, assistant director for museum programs at the historical society, served as project director and curator of the exhibition. As always, he and his staff proved themselves first-rate scholars and museum professionals. Trustee William B. Thalhimer III provided key assistance in the early stages of the project. S. Sidney and Anne H. Meyers, the Honorable Ezra and Katherine Meyers Cohen, and Michael and Nancy Meyers Marsiglia provided financial support for the publication of this catalog in memory of Naomi S. Cohn and Selma Cohn Meyers. Last, but certainly not least, I offer my sincere thanks to the Jewish Community Federation of Richmond, the Virginia Foundation for the Humanities and Public Policy, and the dozens of very generous people who made significant financial contributions to this project. My warmest appreciation is extended to them, as well as to all of the people and institutions who have made "Commonwealth and Community" possible.

CHARLES F. BRYAN, JR.
Director, Virginia Historical Society

PREFACE

In the late afternoon of 13 July 1994, lightning struck a transformer on the roof of St. James's Episcopal Church in Richmond. Within minutes flames had spread throughout the eighty-two-year-old structure, causing extensive damage but not destroying the building. Even as firemen dampened down the smoldering ashes, Barry Hofheimer, president of Congregation Beth Ahabah, located a few doors down on Franklin Street, arrived to offer the use of the synagogue sanctuary by the parishioners of St. James's until they could rebuild.

Although some people extolled Beth Ahabah's offer as a mark of goodwill, the members of neither congregation saw it as unusual. The two congregations, one Jewish and the other Episcopalian, had long been good neighbors. They shared a parking lot and cooperated in social service programs. Over the years the rabbis of Beth Ahabah and the ministers of St. James's had often exchanged pulpits. The members of Beth Ahabah were glad to do the neighborly thing, and the members of St. James's, while certainly grateful, accepted the overture in the spirit in which it had been extended. A few months later, the Reverend Robert H. Trache, the senior rector of St. James's, spoke at a Friday evening service in the synagogue, and in his comments he noted that it was getting hard to tell whether they were now in "St. Ahabah" or "Beth James's."

Hofheimer's offer was not the first of its kind in the history of the Jews of Virginia. On 12 February 1916, fire destroyed the Italian Renaissance–style temple of Ohef Sholom in Norfolk, and the following day all of the churches in the area offered their buildings to the congregation to use while it rebuilt. In Alexandria, congregations have always enjoyed the hospitality of nearby Christian churches to accommodate overflowing High Holiday crowds, as well as during renovations and construction.

The significance of the Beth Ahabah–St. James's story and that of Ohef Sholom is that in many ways they symbolize much of Jewish history in the commonwealth. Although there have been instances of both overt and covert anti-Semitism (in the spring of 1996 vandals defaced several synagogues in Richmond; a few years earlier there had been similar incidents in northern Virginia), for the most part Jews have found a welcoming home in the Old Dominion, and their history goes back to the very origins of Virginia.

What is unusual about Jewish history here is how very usual it is. Jews were involved in the early settlement of the colony; they farmed, traded, explored, fought in the Revolution, struggled successfully alongside other non-Anglicans for religious freedom, owned slaves, joined their neighbors in supporting the Confederacy, and in general have shared the ups and downs of Virginia for nearly four centuries.

This is not to say that Jewish history has perfectly tracked Virginia history at all times. In this century the Holocaust and the State of Israel have had special meaning to American Jews, but here again, the understanding and support evinced by Virginians of all faiths have affirmed that Jews are part and parcel of the ongoing history of the commonwealth.

For the past four centuries, Virginia Jews have fought in all wars in which the Old Dominion has participated and have contributed to the prosperity of the commonwealth as a whole and to the well-being of individual cities and towns. They have held elected and appointed office, ranging from local council members and mayors to members of the General Assembly and Congress. They have served as volunteers and leaders of public enterprises, and, perhaps most important of all, they have been neighbors.

They have done so not as a despised minority cravenly seeking tolerance but as proud citizens of the state. They have been, as one observer noted, "a part but not apart" from the history of Virginia. Aside from their religious beliefs, there is little to distinguish Virginia Jews from their Christian neighbors. The message of this exhibit is that nearly all Virginians have seen this as the way it should be.

Many people assisted in the preparation of this catalog. Robert I. Urofsky was immensely helpful as a research assistant, spending countless hours in the Virginia Historical Society's library and other archival collections. I am also grateful to the following for their help in locating information and objects: Shirley S. Belkowitz, archivist of the Congregation Beth Ahabah Museum and Archives; Jennifer Gregory Priest, archivist of Temple Ohef Sholom in Norfolk; Joseph T. Rainer of Richmond; Suzanne Savery of Petersburg; Judy Sieff and Linda Marshall of Congregation Rodef Shalom in Falls Church; and the staffs of the American Jewish Archives in Cincinnati and the American Jewish Historical Society in Waltham, Massachusetts. The manuscript benefited from the comments of Ruth Sinberg Baker of Alexandria; SueAnn Bangel of Newport News; Cynthia N. Krumbein, former archivist at the Congregation Beth Ahabah Museum and Archives; Claire M. Rosenbaum of Richmond; Roseann Schewel of Lynchburg; Robert I. Urofsky; Saul Viener of Richmond; and Stephen Whitfield of Brandeis University.

MELVIN I. UROFSKY

BEGINNINGS

THE history of Jews in Virginia is as old as the history of the commonwealth itself. Joachim Gaunse (or Jacob Gans), a Prague metallurgist, crossed the ocean in 1585 as part of Sir Walter Ralegh's ill-fated Roanoke expedition, the first English effort to colonize the New World. When the English tried again in the early seventeenth century, settlers arriving in Jamestown on the *Abigail* in 1621 included thirty-eight-year-old Elias Legardo. For most of the next century and a half, one finds references to individual Jews dotted throughout the Old Dominion's history. John Levy, for example, received a patent for 200 acres on the main branch of Powell's Creek in James City County in 1648. David Ferera, a resident of New Amsterdam, was engaged in the tobacco trade by 1658 and may have visited Virginia on business. In York County, Moses Nehemiah found himself involved in a lawsuit in 1658. In the middle of the century we also find references to Sephardic Jews (those who came from the Iberian peninsula), such as the brothers Silvedo and Manuel Rodriguez in Lancaster County. There are no records of a Jewish community—as opposed to individuals—until the eve of the American Revolution.

Virginia throughout its colonial era remained overwhelmingly agricultural, a land of large plantations. Under restrictions imposed by the imperial mercantile system, the planters had to sell their tobacco primarily to English and Scottish agents licensed to engage in the import-export trade; similarly, they bought most of the goods they needed directly from London merchants. Despite the presence of a great natural harbor at the mouth of the James, Virginia never developed the commerce that marked Boston, New York, Philadelphia, or Charleston. There were no cities in the colony; the capital at Williamsburg was little more than a large village and Richmond before the Revolution even smaller. Not until the nineteenth century did Virginia have a town boasting 5,000 inhabitants. The Jews who migrated to the British colonies in the seventeenth and eighteenth centuries had no experience as farmers; they had been merchants or artisans in the Old World and looked for places where they could set up shop and ply the trades or crafts they knew. To succeed, they needed commercial centers, of which none then existed in Virginia.

Although Jews enjoyed more rights in the British colonies than they did almost anywhere else in the world at that time, they still suffered restrictions. At no time in the colonial period did Jews enjoy equal status with their Christian neighbors. In seventeenth-century Virginia, naturalization involved taking oaths, and because Jews could not profess faith in Jesus or take the sacrament, they found themselves ineligible for both citizenship and public office, as well as attendance at the College of William and Mary. In 1705 the General Assembly specifically excluded non-Christians, along with blacks, Catholics, and convicts, from testifying as witnesses in court. Denial of the Trinity in Anglican Virginia led to the loss of civil rights and could subject offenders to imprisonment.

Although they were as anti-Catholic as they were anti-Jewish, the colony's leaders had no hesitation in borrowing a medieval church rule that prohibited Jews from employing Christian indentured servants. When the Lords Commissioners for Trade and Plantations issued a patent for land in the western part of the colony in 1733, the document provided for "an Unlimited Liberty of Conscience . . . of all Religions excepting Heathens, Jews and Papists who are to be utterly disqualified and for ever excluded from holding any office of Trust or Profit." Parliament passed the Naturalization Act of 1740, which made Jews in the colonies eligible for citizenship, but there is no record that any Jew availed himself of this right. Throughout the colonial era, the established church in the colony stood strongly against granting any rights to Jews.

The Anglican church opposed any nonconforming sect, and all the residents of the colony, whether Anglican or not, had to pay taxes to support the church. Non-Anglican clergy often found themselves forbidden to speak or write on religious questions, and just two and a half years before the Declaration of Independence, James Madison raged to a friend about the "diabolical, Hell-conceived principles of persecution" then abroad in Virginia. "There are at this [time] in the adjacent county not less than five or six well-meaning men [Baptists] in close gaol for publishing their religious sentiments." As the late dean of American Jewish historians, Jacob Rader Marcus, commented, "[I]t is therefore hardly likely, in a colony where almost every Protestant Dissenter had to fight for toleration, that Jews would be encouraged to come in and would receive religious and political privileges."

In Virginia as elsewhere, however, a strong discrepancy existed between laws and practice. To begin with, just as in the New England colonies, a strong interest in Hebraism existed in Virginia. William Byrd II, George Wythe, and Richard Lee II studied Hebrew, and young Virginia gentlemen could secure instruction in the sacred language at James Waddell's school in Lancaster County. Moreover, the Hebraic tradition as found in the King James Bible exercised a strong and enduring influence throughout the southern colonies. Although one cannot deny the existence of anti-Jewish prejudices and legal disabilities, they apparently proved neither debilitating nor of great inconvenience.

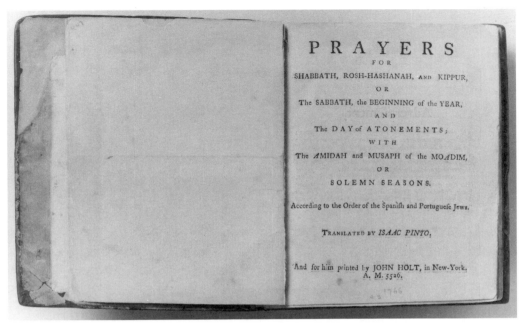

American Jewish Historical Society, Waltham, Massachusetts; photograph courtesy of the Valentine Museum, Richmond

Judaism is a communal religion and calls for its adherents to pray in a *minyan*, a religious quorum of ten adults. This early prayer book was published in New York in 1766.

Despite the existence of established churches in nearly all the British colonies, a plenitude of religious sects could be found everywhere. European-style anti-Semitism did not travel well across the Atlantic. Although restrictions against Jews remained on the statute books of several colonies—including Virginia—until well after the Revolution, it appears that in everyday life these laws often had little effect. Jews continued to immigrate to the New World, and eighteenth-century records show Jews owning land, engaging in lawsuits, and doing business in Virginia.

By these records we know that Moses Nehemiah was discharged from debt in York County in 1658 and that Thomas Jacobs sued Robert Cousens in Prince George County in 1738. The first Jews in Charlottesville arrived in 1757, when Michael Israel and his wife, Sarah, patented eighty acres in North Garden near the pass through the mountains between North Garden and Batesville, a pass that has ever since been known as Israel's Gap. When George Washington led an expedition across the Allegheny Mountains in 1754 to warn the French away from the Falls of the Ohio, Michael Franks and Jacob Myer accompanied him.

Jewish merchants in Philadelphia and New York held stock in the land companies that opened up the western part of the colony and often sent their agents to help explore the region. The fur traders of Lancaster relied heavily on a man known only as Levy, a partner and agent of Joseph Simon who led trading expeditions out of Winchester as far north as present-day Detroit, then still part of Virginia. Court records indicate Jews living in the area that is now West Virginia at least as early as 1749. Peter Hitt's account book showed a Mr. Lipsheim in Fauquier County as early as 1758. In Williamsburg there lived Dr. John de Sequeyra, who is credited by Thomas Jefferson with introducing the custom of eating tomatoes, which had before then been grown only as ornamental plants.

We also know of Dr. Isaac Levy, who practiced his trade in the far western part of Virginia then known as the Illinois Country. In addition to medicine, Levy also engaged in commerce and figures frequently in the court records of the early 1780s. In one case he sued a Mr. Buteau for not paying for physician's services. Buteau answered that he had not been cured, whereupon the court ordered Levy to continue treating his patient but also instructed Buteau to follow the doctor's orders. Soon after, Levy came back to the judge and complained that Buteau had disobeyed him. The court summoned Buteau, who explained that he had taken the sixty pills Levy had prescribed in two days, instead of over an eight-day period, so he could get well more speedily. Levy responded that this dosage would have been impossible, because that quantity of pills would have killed the patient. The court ordered Buteau to pay Levy's bill.

The absence of communities, more than any other element, retarded Jewish migration into the colony. Judaism is a communal religion, and nearly all of its commandments and religious tenets deal with how one treats others. Although Jews may, when necessary, say their daily devotions alone, tradition calls for them to pray in a *minyan*, a group of ten adults (Orthodox congregations still restrict the *minyan* to ten men). This core value of community dates back more than three millennia. According to the Torah, when God gave the Ten Commandments to the Israelites at Mount Sinai, their response was not individual—"I will do and I will hear"—but rather communal—*Na'aseh v'Nishmah*—"We will do and we will hear."

By the second half of the eighteenth century, individual Jews could be found in the Tidewater, Fredericksburg, Richmond, Petersburg, and Albemarle County. No nucleus, no stable entity around which a community could grow, existed, however. But grand events were astir, as the colonies prepared to declare their independence from Great Britain. In Virginia especially, a great burst of freedom provided the ideal climate in which that nucleus, and others like it, could grow.

At the time of the American Revolution, there were about two thousand Jews in the thirteen British colonies. Although it is impossible to determine

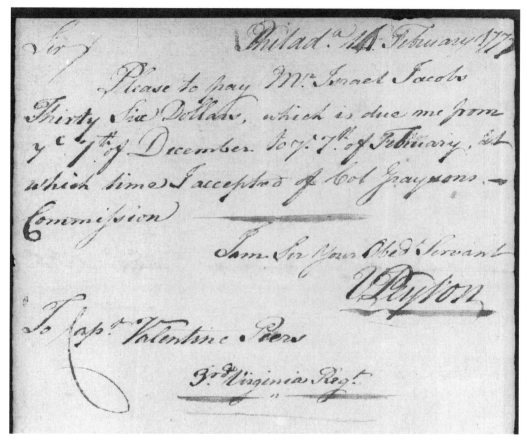

In February 1777, Valentine Peyton (1756–1815) of the Third Virginia Regiment asked his captain to pay money owed him to Israel Jacobs, a Jewish merchant in Philadelphia.

on which side the men fought, the research indicates that for the most part, colonial Jews cast their lots with the patriots. Some gained renown, such as New York financier Haym Salomon. A few, such as Moses Myers of Norfolk, held the rank of officer, but the majority were enlisted men. Some Jewish merchants, such as the Gratzes in Virginia, are in the record books as having secured commodities for the state government, and some also helped the Continental forces secure supplies. Here again, however, little could differentiate Jewish merchants in this activity from their gentile counterparts.

As historian Samuel Rezneck points out, it was important that Jews, given the small size of the community, did their share for independence. They were visibly present and could not and would not be overlooked by the colonial leaders. Moreover, by fighting alongside their Christian neighbors, Jews could legitimately demand equality of treatment, not as charity but as a right. When the citizens of Henrico County sent a remonstrance to the state legislature on 11 June 1783, declaring that they had risked everything dear to them in the struggle against Britain, the name of Isaiah Isaacs was listed with the others. He, like they, had risked his life, his fortune, and his sacred honor, and he expected to receive, not a monetary reward, but equality before the law.

On 12 June 1776, three weeks before the Continental Congress issued the Declaration of Independence, the Virginia revolutionary convention adopted a declaration of rights, one that in substance was copied by nearly every other state and that eventually formed a model for the federal Bill of Rights. Section one held that "all Men are by nature equally free and Independent and have certain inherent Rights." Section sixteen declared "That Religion or the Duty which we owe to our Creator and the manner of discharging it can be directed only by reason and Conviction not by force

Collection of Norman Flayderman

Brothers Barnard and Michael Gratz of Philadelphia expanded their trading to Fredericksburg and Williamsburg in 1776 and throughout the Revolution kept Virginia supplied by running the British blockade. By 1783, Michael Gratz had moved to Virginia but later returned to Philadelphia. The Gratz brothers received a grant from Governor Patrick Henry for land in Montgomery County in February 1786.

or Violence and therefore all Men are equally intitled to the free exercise of Religion according to the Dictates of Conscience and that it is the mutual Duty of all to practice Christian Forbearance Love and Charity towards each other."

Although noble in sentiment, the section had no force. It did not abolish any of the legal liabilities then still on the books that inhibited not only Jews and Muslims but dissenting Christian sects as well. The incorporation of the Declaration of Rights into the new state constitution on 29 June elevated the status of section sixteen, but in effect it remained little more than a pious platitude. In one important respect, however, the statement did mark a significant step forward in the march toward religious liberty in Virginia and then in the nation. The original wording of section sixteen had spoken of "tolerance," with its implied derogation of the minority sect as inferior. Thanks to James Madison, who clearly understood the unpleasant connotations of the word, the final draft provided, at least in theory, for the possibility of true religious liberty. Moreover, the new constitution did relieve dissenting groups, such as the Presbyterians and Baptists, of limits that had been imposed by acts of Parliament, which no longer applied in Virginia, and also exempted them from paying taxes to support the Anglican church, which remained established although deprived of some of its revenues. It soon became evident, however, that the assembly had no wish to remove further restrictions.

Legislation to encourage the immigration and naturalization of dissenting religious groups, including Jews, came before the Virginia House of Delegates in autumn 1776. Thomas Jefferson, who drafted the proposed act, emphasized the benefits these groups would confer on the commonwealth and affirmed his confidence that Jews would be good citizens. The bill never came to a vote. The Anglican church still possessed great influence and for another decade remained the established religion of the state. Jews and certain other sects could not even legally conduct marriage ceremonies until 1784.

Although the small number of Jews could not secure more liberal laws, the far larger number of Baptists and Presbyterians could and did demand religious freedom. Eventually their claims prevailed. At the end of 1776 the legislature, without explicitly disestablishing the Anglican church, repealed all of the statutes that enforced and supported its position. Deprived of these bulwarks, the Anglicans soon became one more of several large Protestant groups in the state. But what about the Jews?

In 1779 the General Assembly received two bills concerning religious liberty. One, entitled "A Bill concerning Religion," would have declared Christianity to be the "established religion" of Virginia and would have required members of individual churches to subscribe to enumerated articles of faith in order for their church to receive a state charter. Each chartered church would receive a share of the tax proceeds, and individuals could designate to which church they wanted their taxes directed. In contrast, Thomas Jefferson's Bill for Religious Freedom would have proclaimed that "no man shall be compelled to frequent or support any religious worship, place or ministry whatsoever."

Neither bill could muster a majority. Then in 1784 Patrick Henry introduced a new assessment bill, this time with the support of the Presbyterian clergy, who appreciated the idea of receiving state tax funds. If adopted, Beverley Randolph told James Madison, the bill would "mean that Turks, Jews and infidels were to contribute to the support of a religion whose truth they did not acknowledge."

Madison managed to delay a vote on the measure, which probably had the support of a majority of the legislature, and in 1785 published his powerful "Memorial and Remonstrance against Religious Assessments." The document rallied the proponents of religious liberty, who flooded the assembly with petitions against the assessment bill. In 1779, for example, a petition from Amherst County favoring assessment had stated that although Catholics ought to be given a "guarded & limited" toleration, they, along with "Jew[s], Turk[s] and Infidel[s]" had to be excluded from holding public office. In 1785 a petition from Chesterfield County complained of the injustice wrought on non-Christians and urged that "Jews, Mehametans and Christians of every Denomination" be made welcome in Virginia. At the next election the voters returned a majority in the assembly opposed to assessment.

The stage was set for Madison to shepherd through one of the great documents of religious freedom in this or any other country, Thomas Jefferson's Virginia Statute for Religious Freedom. The bill expressly declared that no man should be forced to support religion. The practice of religion should be a private matter dependent on an individual's own free will. The statute did not distinguish between Jews and Christians, or among Christian sects. Years later Jefferson noted that a final attempt had been made to amend the preamble to the bill to identify "Almighty God . . . the holy author of our religion" with Jesus Christ, but the effort failed. Jefferson also made clear that he and Madison had intended the statute to cover all groups, "to comprehend within the mantle of [the act's] protection the Jew and the Gentile, the Christian and Mahometan, the Hindoo, and infidel of every denomination."

The Virginia statute of 1786, which remains the first provision of the laws of Virginia, gave Jews and other minority sects complete religious freedom. It marked the penultimate step in separating church and state in Virginia; all that remained was for the legislature to repeal existing laws in conflict with the statute, which it did in 1798 and 1799. In 1802 all religious bodies received equality of rights. Although Jefferson and Madison both

Collection of Norman Flayderman

Among the forty-five signatories of the articles of incorporation of the United Illinois and Ouabashe land companies on 29 April 1780 were five prominent American Jews and five signers of the Declaration of Independence. Virginia, however, claimed the Illinois Country and had created it a county two years earlier. The Old Dominion relinquished its claims to Congress in 1784 only on condition that all prior land sales, such as those of the Illinois and Ouabashe land companies, be null and void.

had Jewish acquaintances, the liberal measures of 1776 and 1786 were not "Jew bills," such as the one in Maryland aimed specifically at repealing restrictions on Jews. The two men strongly believed that religion should be a private matter and that every person ought to have full liberty of conscience. This attitude meant that Jews and other small groups would not have to depend on the toleration of the majority but would be entitled, along with every other religious group, to full equality before the law. In the long history of Jewish persecution, such freedom had rarely been enjoyed. The Virginia Statute for Religious Freedom turned up a fertile soil in which Jewish communities could flourish and prosper. The initial evidence of that growth came in the state's capital, Richmond.

The first Jew to settle permanently in Richmond appears to have been a silversmith, Isaiah Isaacs; he was in the colony at least as early as 1769, because in that year a London creditor dunned him for a debt. Sometime toward the end of the Revolution, Isaacs entered into a partnership with Jacob I. Cohen, who had joined the rebel forces in South Carolina, fought creditably, and had been captured, but who had then escaped from the British to settle in Richmond.

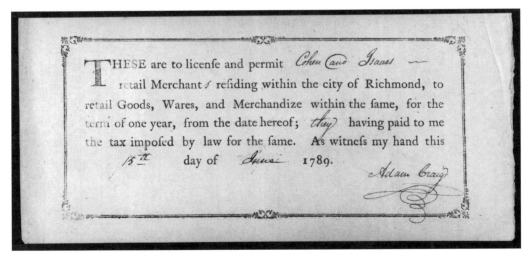

Collection of Norman Flayderman

Silversmith Isaiah Isaacs (1747–1806), perhaps the first Jew in Richmond, arrived in 1769; his business partner, Jacob I. Cohen (1744–1823), came to Virginia during the American Revolution. Known throughout the commonwealth as "the Jews' store," their retail firm carried a variety of provisions and also sold real estate. This business license dates from June 1789.

The firm of Cohen & Isaacs soon became one of the most prosperous in town. Primarily merchants, the two men, like most other businessmen and planters of this period, speculated in real estate, and records indicate that Isaacs held parcels in Richmond and Norfolk and in Henrico, Powhatan, Albemarle, and Louisa counties, as well as part ownership in a large tract of land—more than 12,000 acres—in the Great Dismal Swamp enterprise. In 1781 Cohen and Isaacs hired Daniel Boone to survey some tracts for them.

They also owned the Bird in Hand, possibly the first inn and tavern in Richmond. A newspaper of the time described this establishment "at the foot of Church Hill. . . . It has every necessary outhouse and a good garden . . . [and] is fitted for two tenements, as stores." They settled the Bird in Hand on their junior partner, Jacob Mordecai, when he married Judith Myers, the daughter of the noted New York silversmith Myer Myers.

Isaacs's entrance into the political arena in the early 1780s indicates that even before the enactment of the Virginia Statute for Religious Freedom the restrictions on Jews seeking civil and military office had little practical force. Isaacs, although unsuccessful in his first bid to sit on the common council, was named clerk of the market in 1785 and later held posts as a tax assessor and a council member.

Isaacs used Hebraic script both when signing his name and when setting important information on paper; his command of written English may have been poor. Like many successful Virginians of the time, he owned slaves, but the spirit of liberty that had allowed him to live freely and to prosper led him to make the following provision in his will:

> Being of opinion that all men are by nature equally free, and being possessed of some of those beings who are unfortunate, doomed to slavery, . . . I must enjoin upon my executor a strict observance of the following clause in my will. My slaves hereafter named are to be and they are hereby manumeted and made free, so that after the different periods hereafter mentioned they shall enjoy all the privileges and immunities of freed people. . . . Each one of my slaves is to receive the value of twenty dollars in clothing on the days of their manumission.

Cohen and Isaacs no doubt knew Joseph Darmstadt, a Hessian sutler who had been taken prisoner at the battle of Saratoga and who had been brought to Virginia as a captive. A number of Hessians were, in fact, Jews forced into service as mercenaries by the German princes, and many of them escaped while in service or chose to stay in this land of freedom after the end of hostilities.

Despite the circumstances of his arrival in the Old Dominion, Darmstadt determined to remain. German farmers in the Shenandoah Valley found his fluency in German an asset, and as a result of their patronage, he prospered as a middleman in Richmond. He lured local businessmen,

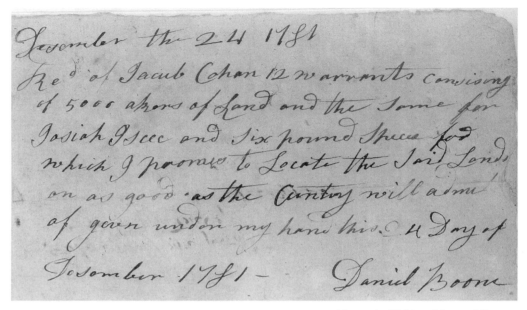

Manuscript Division, Library of Congress

The Richmond firm of Cohen & Isaacs cashed in on the brisk business in land warrants at the close of the Revolution. On Christmas Eve in 1781, they commissioned Daniel Boone to locate 10,000 acres for them in Kentucky.

lawyers, doctors, and others to his home and business near Market Square every morning by personally brewing a large pot of coffee. Darmstadt's soon became the Richmond center for collecting the latest news and gossip.

Two brothers, Marcus and Lyon (Lionel) Elcan, came to Virginia from Prussia sometime in the early 1780s. Lyon married Elizabeth Hooper of Buckingham County, where he established his residence. Marcus opened a dry goods store in Richmond, and one of his advertisements indicates a variety of goods available that might make a modern department store envious—clothing, fabrics, furniture, saddles, pewter, pots and pans, dishes, lead shot, powder, wine, salt, and "a number of other articles too tedious to mention, which he will sell for CASH, COUNTRY PRODUCE, and PUBLIC SECURITIES on very moderate terms." Marcus Elcan became wealthy from his business and land dealings, and like other Richmond Jews, he joined the Masons and participated in local civic affairs.

Many Jews, not only those in Virginia, joined the Masonic order. They found the Freemasons congenial philosophically, in part because the Masons accepted the Jewish date for the creation of the world, 3760 B.C.E. There also existed a widespread belief that in times of trouble, Masons helped each other, and there are numerous stories of Jews and others in peril who were saved by fellow Masons. That commercial benefits might accrue from these contacts no doubt appealed to some members, Jew and

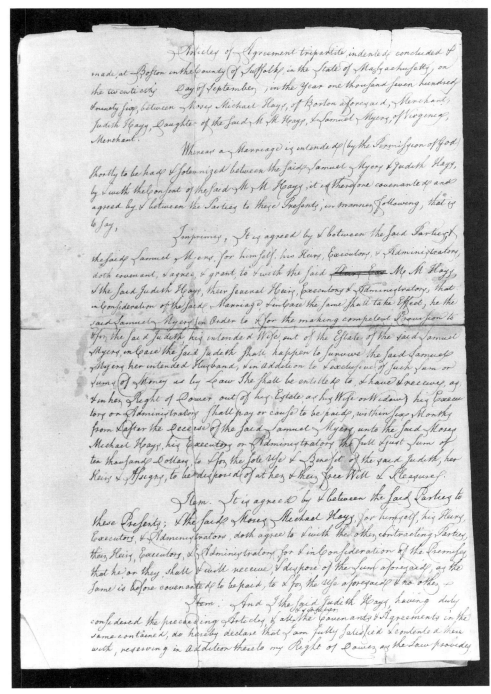

Myers Family Papers, 1739–1805, Virginia Historical Society

Moses Michael Hays, a wealthy Boston merchant, and Samuel Myers (1755–1836) of Petersburg entered into a prenuptial agreement on 29 September 1796 before Myers's marriage to Hays's daughter, Judith (1767–1844). The agreement was modeled on the *ketubah*, the traditional Jewish marriage contract.

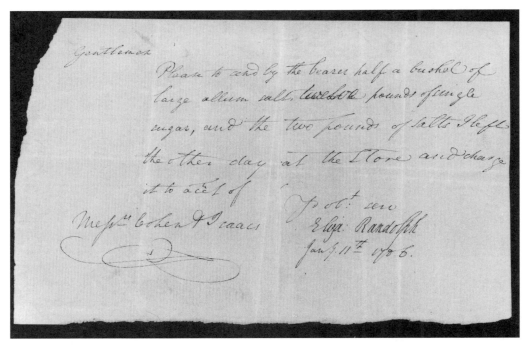

Elizabeth Nicholas Randolph (1753–1810) placed an order for salts and sugar with Cohen & Isaacs in January 1786. Later that year, her husband became Virginia's governor.

non-Jew alike, but of far greater importance, Masonry believed and acted on principles of tolerance and social equality. Whatever their individual religious beliefs, Masons extended to Jews not only the opportunity to become members, but also, once they had been accepted within the order, to be treated as equals, as human beings. As a number of commentators have noted, the order embodied in the fullest the aspirations of English rationalism and French humanitarianism. This respect meant a great deal to Jews in the New World and the Old. To people starved for social acceptance, Masonry provided an opportunity, at least within a fraternity that aspired to universal brotherhood.

About the same time as Cohen, Isaacs, and Darmstadt were prospering in Richmond, a connection formed with the growing port of Norfolk. Samuel and Moses Myers had been perhaps the largest Jewish mercantile house in New York during the 1770s but had gone bankrupt in the economic upheaval following the war. They needed a new venue in which to conduct business, and to find one Moses traveled south. In December 1786 he wrote to Samuel, then in Amsterdam trying to collect some of their old debts, that "in Virginia, money is yet to be made, as it is in both Charleston and Georgia." Moses may have originally decided to settle in

Because Freemasons held and acted on principles of tolerance and social equality, many Jews found Masonry congenial. This gold Masonic pin was presented to Abraham Gunst by members of his lodge "as a token of Esteem, Richmond, Va., June 24, 1874."

Beth Ahabah Museum and Archives

Richmond, but a business dispute with Jacob Mordecai, as well as a warehouse fire in Richmond in which Myers lost some merchandise, led him to settle on Norfolk. There Moses became one of the town's most prosperous and influential figures; he built a magnificent Federal mansion that was for many years a showplace and is now maintained as part of the Chrysler Museum. Samuel Myers moved first to Petersburg and then on to Richmond, where he opened a branch of the business. The Myers firm carried on extensive business dealings with northern merchants and was in effect an agent of the important Philadelphia commercial house of Stephen Girard.

How much the spirit of liberty affected Virginia Jewry can be seen in the case of Judah Moses, a Richmond merchant who had been born in Posen. Prussia had long been angling to enter the American market but could not do so while Great Britain controlled the colonies and enforced its mercantile restrictions. Following the Revolution, Prussia signed a treaty of commerce and amity that Congress ratified in May 1786. The following spring, Moses approached the Prussian government in Berlin with an offer: he would barter American raw materials, primarily Virginia tobacco, for

Moses Myers (1753–1835), shown here in a portrait by Gilbert Stuart painted in 1803–4, was Norfolk's superintendent of the Bank of Richmond, a member of the common council, and personal agent of Thomas Jefferson. His magnificent Federal house in Norfolk, shown below, is now operated by the Chrysler Museum.

Chrysler Museum of Art, Norfolk, Virginia

Virginia Historical Society

German manufactures such as textiles, hardware, and porcelain. Although the proposal received serious consideration from the German civil servants in the department of commerce and manufacture, for unknown reasons it was never implemented.

What is interesting is that at this time Prussia still imposed strict restrictions on its Jewish population and even allowed cities to exclude them altogether. Not until 1871 would the Jews of Germany finally be emancipated and given equal rights. But in 1787, a Virginia Jew, Judah Moses, insisted that he be treated by the Prussian government not as a German Jew under disabilities, but as an American citizen, entitled to all the rights that status bestowed on Jew and gentile alike.

Of course, not all Jews who settled in Virginia proved as fortunate as the merchants. Meyer Derkheim, an itinerant *mohel* (ritual circumciser) had so little business that he had to make his living as a candlemaker. The

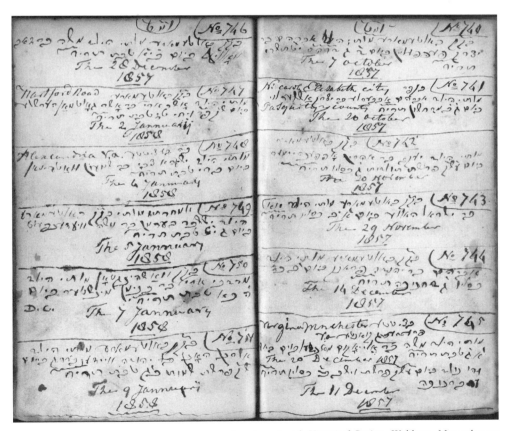

American Jewish Historical Society, Waltham, Massachusetts

M. S. Polack, a Baltimore *mohel*, traveled to Alexandria, Elizabeth City County, Charlottesville, Winchester, and other Virginia towns to perform circumcisions according to Jewish law. His accounts for 1857–58, kept in a mix of Hebrew and English, read from right to left.

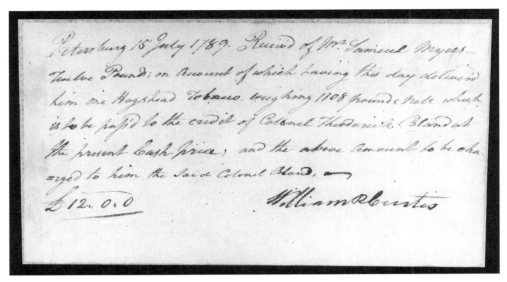

Theodorick Bland (1742–1790) of Petersburg received £12 from Samuel Myers on 15 July 1789 for one hogshead of tobacco.

Richmond city fathers took pity on the impoverished man and made him one of the capital's lamplighters.

The Jews who lived in Richmond and other parts of Virginia seemed not to have suffered from either social anti-Semitism or legal restrictions on their political and economic rights. They participated not only in the affairs of their religious community but also on the wider public stage. Many joined the Richmond Light Infantry Blues, the Masons, and other civic groups. Zalma Rehiné was a founder of the Blues, and Solomon Jacobs, who served for a time as Richmond's mayor, also took part. Joseph Darmstadt held the office of grand treasurer of the Grand Lodge of Virginia Masons at the same time that John Marshall, chief justice of the United States, was the grand master. In 1788 sixty Richmonders formed the Amicable Society, which engaged in charitable work. John Marshall belonged, as did Joseph Darmstadt, Samuel Myers, and other Jews.

By 1790, there were about 3,000 Jews in the United States, of whom roughly 200 lived in Virginia. Norfolk had at least one family, and Petersburg had ten or twelve individuals. David Isaacs, the younger brother of Isaiah Isaacs, had a store on Main Street in Charlottesville. Dr. Isaac Levy practiced medicine in the wild region known as the Illinois Country. Hezekiah Levy was a member of the Fredericksburg Lodge of Masons No. 4, to which George Washington belonged.

Richmond, however, had become the center of Jewish life in the state. When Richmond incorporated as a city in 1782, the census listed three Jewish residents, although the records indicate that more than three Jewish families lived there at the time. The 1790 census listed twenty-eight adult Jewish males out of a total of 171 white males over age twenty-one. Because some of these men had wives and family, the city's Jewish population probably exceeded 100, at a time when Richmond had a total population estimated at between 1,200 and 1,800, of whom half were slaves. The time had come to form a congregation and build a synagogue.

"TO BIGOTRY NO SANCTION"

In 1789, the same year that George Washington first took the oath of office as president of the United States under its new Constitution, the Jews of Richmond formed their first synagogue, K'hal Kadosh Beth Shalome—the Holy Congregation of the House of Peace. The two events are not unrelated. The political climate of the United States was already freer and more welcoming to Jews and other small religious sects than that of Europe. The Founding Fathers of the new nation seemed determined to avoid the religious discrimination and persecution that had been hallmarks of European history for more than a thousand years. When the Jewish community of Newport, Rhode Island, sent the hero of the Revolution congratulations on his assuming the presidency, Washington responded in words that thrilled Jews throughout the thirteen states:

> It is now no more that toleration is spoken of as if it was by the indulgence of one class of people that another enjoyed the exercise of their inherent natural rights. For happily the Government of the United States, which gives to bigotry no sanction, to persecution no assistance, requires only that they who live under its protection should demean themselves as good citizens, in giving it on all occasions their effectual support. . . . May the Children of the Stock of Abraham, who dwell in this land, continue to merit and enjoy the good will of the other inhabitants, while every one shall sit in safety under his own vine and fig tree and there shall be none to make him afraid.

In one statement, Washington, who more than any other man symbolized the new nation, affirmed not only the principle of religious freedom but also the fact that Jews were citizens—the first time that a modern head of state had ever uttered such a sentiment. It is not surprising that American Jews began to refer to their new home as a second Jerusalem. For the Jews of Virginia, still exultant over the 1786 Statute for Religious Freedom, such sentiments reinforced their feelings of belonging, and they began to think in terms of permanency, of putting down roots, of building a synagogue.

The synagogue, as historian Jacob Rader Marcus noted, constituted "the primary institution in the American Jewish community." During the colonial era, except in such cities as New York or Philadelphia, there were rarely enough Jews to support a permanent congregation. Individual Jews who came to a town frequently intermarried if they stayed, and their Jewishness disappeared. But for there to be enough Jews not only to form the *minyan*, the ritual quorum, but also to support a synagogue suggested not only permanence in residency, but also a belief that they could survive as a Jewish community. As Marcus saw it, the synagogue "is the synthesizing factor in the writing of the history of American Jewry; it is the spinal cord of American Jewish life." The importance of the synagogue derived not only from its locus as a house of prayer but also from its functional service as the center of communal life. The early history of Beth Shalome illustrates this centrality well.

The Jews of Richmond apparently had been holding prayer services in various homes from 1786 or 1787, but there had been no formal structure, no leader, and no permanent place of worship. On a Sunday afternoon, 24 August 1789, twenty-nine men, evidently the entire adult male Jewish population of Richmond, gathered to create the first Jewish congregation in Virginia's capital and the sixth in the United States. Jacob I. Cohen, probably the wealthiest and most prominent member of the community, appears to have taken a major role in calling the meeting, which then elected Marcus Elcan as president. In their constitution, the founders declared that "we, the subscribers of the Israelite religion in this place, desirous of promoting the divine worship, which, by the blessings of God has been transmitted by our ancestors, have this day agreed to form ourselves into a society for the better effecting the said laudable purposes

American Jewish Archives, Cincinnati

K'hal Kadosh Beth Shalome, the first Jewish congregation in Richmond, built its synagogue in 1822. The building was demolished in 1934.

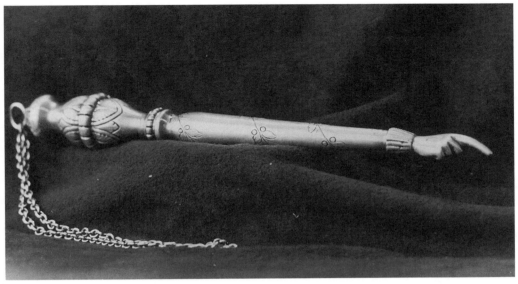

Beth Ahabah Museum and Archives

The *yad* (hand) is a pointer used by the reader of the Torah in a synagogue so that he can follow the text without touching the sacred scroll with his bare hands. This coin silver one, by Richmond Jew Lewis Hyman, was made for K'hal Kadosh Beth Shalome about 1850.

Henry Hyman, whose brother Lewis also was a silversmith, advertised his trade in the Richmond city directory in 1850.

Beth Ahabah Museum and Archives

to be known and distinguished in Israel by the name of B'eth Shalom." Unlike the earlier congregations of New York and Philadelphia, the founders of Beth Shalome did not demand ritual observance by its members. The membership requirements precluded indentured servants and slaves but allowed that "every free man residing in this city for the term of three months, of the age of 21 years and who congregates with us, shall be a yahid [member] of the kehilla [congregation] and entitled to every right and privilege of the same."

The founding members of Beth Shalome included a few Sephardic Jews, that is, those who originally came from the Iberian peninsula, but the majority were from England, the Low Countries, and Germany and followed the Ashkenazic or German ritual common to central and eastern Europe. Nonetheless, the Richmond congregation chose to adopt the Sephardic ritual, primarily because the other five organized congregations in the United States all did as well. This conformity would allow Beth Shalome to maintain the closest possible relations with the other communities. (One should not confuse the differences between the Sephardic and Ashkenazic rituals as theological disagreements, such as those that mark today's Reform, Conservative, and Orthodox branches of Judaism. At this time all Jews were "Orthodox," and the differences involved pronunciation of Hebrew, order of prayers, and similar matters of ritual.)

Beth Shalome also adopted the Sephardic form of governance, in which a *parnas* (president) and *junta* (board) governed. Every year, on the Sunday before Rosh Hashanah, the Jewish New Year, the congregation would elect its officials for the coming twelve months. Unlike some of the other congregations, where the *parnas* had punitive authority to impose ritual and rules, the head of Beth Shalome had only nominal authority in this area, and actual governance of the congregation appears to have been fairly democratic, perhaps a result of Virginia's own liberal attitude in religious matters.

The new congregation rented rooms in a three-story brick building on the west side of Nineteenth Street, between Franklin and Grace. Although it was many years before the congregation could afford a full-time rabbi, Isaac H. Judah assumed the post of *hazzan*, or reader. He conducted services in Hebrew, although an English translation was available. The congregation seemed well satisfied with this arrangement and loath to make changes; as late as 1867, the membership voted to retain the Sephardic ritual, although by then nearly all of the congregants could be classified as Ashkenazic.

How quickly Beth Shalome became the community focal point for Richmond's Jews can be seen in several instances. In the fall of 1789, George Washington proclaimed a national day of thanksgiving and requested that all denominations join in the observance. Jacob I. Cohen, who

"A Prayer for the Country," composed by Jacob I. Cohen, a veteran of the American Revolution, was read at Beth Shalome on 26 November 1789. The Richmonder's prayer gave thanks to God for "Send[ing] us a Deliverer in the Head of this Nation the President of the United States."

had fought for the new nation in its Revolutionary War, composed "A Prayer for the Country," which was read in Beth Shalome's meeting rooms on 26 November 1789. The prayer derived some of its phrases from the traditional appeal for the preservation of the civil authority but in other sections seems to have been original. It read, in part:

> O God of Hosts, thou has set peace and tranquillity in our palaces
> And has set the President of the United States as our head. . . .
> May God Almighty hearken to our voice and save us.
> We will prolong our prayer before God, our Redeemer.
> May he guard and keep the Vice President, senators, and representatives of the
> United States.
> May he give good sense and understanding to the officers of the courts.
> May the hearts of our governors be upright and faithful.
> May he prosper and bless our country,
> And deliver us from the hands of outside enemies.

The following year Beth Shalome joined with the congregations of Charleston, New York, and Philadelphia to send a belated letter of congratulations to Washington. In fulsome prose, in which they referred to the president as God's "chosen and beloved servant," the congregations declared that "it is reserved for you to unite in affection for your character and person every political and religious denomination of men, and in this will the Hebrew congregations aforesaid yield to no class of their fellow-citizens." In Washington's reply, he noted that "the liberal sentiment towards each other, which marks every political and religious denomination of men in this country stands unrivalled in the history of nations."

Although couched in the formal style typical of the eighteenth century, Washington's comments did much to establish the notion that the United States, as a nation, stood committed to the same principles that Virginia had adopted in its laws—not toleration, but freedom and equality—principles that received confirmation with the ratification of the First Amendment in 1791. The Richmond congregation's copy of the letter from Washington, one of its most prized possessions, disappeared along with most of Beth Shalome's early records in the great conflagration that destroyed much of Richmond in 1865.

Beth Shalome and its members knew that Jewish communal life involved more than just joining together in prayer. In Europe every Jewish town of any size had a number of educational, philanthropic, and pious associations, and Jewish communities in the New World, even if they could not afford to recreate such an extensive institutional structure, nonetheless recognized the needs that these agencies served.

In 1788 the Amicable Society of Richmond had been founded to "relieve strangers and wayfarers in distress," and its members had included Joseph Darmstadt, Samuel Myers, and other members of the Jewish community. Beth Shalome founded its own Ezrat Orchim society in 1789 to provide help for indigent travelers. Although the rules governing the giving of this aid did not specify that the recipient be Jewish, one can assume that the establishment of the society met the need created by the large number of requests for help addressed to the congregation, probably by Jewish peddlers and other travelers in financial distress. The first president, Isaiah Isaacs, distributed funds according to a constitution that spelled out how much could be given to particular applicants (distinguishing, for example, between "those persons who are of a gentlemanly good character" and those "whose characters are unknown" and between those who had lived in Richmond for at least six months and those who had recently arrived).

Capital Area Preservation at Mordecai Historic Park, Raleigh, North Carolina

Jacob Mordecai (1762–1838), founder of the Warrenton Female Academy in North Carolina, was married to Judith Myers, a sister of merchant Samuel Myers. He was *parnas* (president) of Beth Shalome in Richmond. His brass seal and traveling inkwell were employed frequently in his life as a scholar, educator, and merchant.

The following year, Isaiah Isaacs donated land on the south side of East Franklin Street, between Twentieth and Twenty-first streets, for a Jewish cemetery. By 1816, this plot seems to have been full, and Beth Shalome established a new Jewish cemetery on Shockoe Hill at Fourth Street, the site of the current Hebrew Cemetery of Richmond. Many but not all of those buried in the older field were reinterred in the Fourth Street site. The earlier cemetery became a victim of neglect. When the city paved Franklin Street, it elevated the road surface; shortly after the Civil War, the city ordered the ground to be raised to street level, so the remaining headstones were laid flat and the cemetery filled in with four feet of earth. In May 1866, a reporter for the *Richmond Dispatch* described the area as "a vacant lot,

Founded on 3 May 1789, the Society of Ezrat Orchim in Richmond sought to assist "people of the Jewish Religion . . . in this City whose distressed Circumstances expose them to many difficulties." It was later succeeded by the Hebrew Beneficial Society.

overrun with rank weeds and grass, showing the track of wagons and bearing the hoof-marks of horses. . . . Hundreds of persons pass it by daily, and if they think of it at all, it is as a piece of waste land, most unaccountably allowed to remain in a useless and neglected condition."

The land did not remain vacant long; the parcel next to it served as the site of a blacksmith's shop and later as a coal yard, and in both instances the owners threw their refuse over the wall. Then in 1909 the community repossessed the parcel, had the trash removed and the plot fenced in, and marked it as the first Jewish cemetery in Richmond. In 1955, as part of the celebration commemorating the 300th anniversary of Jewish life in America, the Franklin Street Cemetery, as it is now called, was reconsecrated.

No records had survived to indicate who was buried there. In 1976, under the supervision of Fred Windmueller, one of the founders of the Beth Ahabah Museum and Archives, excavations in the fenced-in section located headstones, many of which still had legible inscriptions. The first two stones belonged to Israel I. Cohen, who had died in 1803, and his sister-in-law, Hester (Esther) Cohen, who had died the following year.

As it happens, an interesting story is connected with the romance and marriage of Esther and Jacob I. Cohen. Born Elizabeth Whitlock in England, she had converted to Judaism in her teens (changing her name to Esther) and then had married the much older Moses Mordecai, who brought his new bride to Philadelphia. Cohen had met her there shortly after he had been repatriated as a prisoner of war. Mordecai died in 1781, and Cohen, renewing his acquaintance with the attractive widow, proposed to marry her the following year.

But men named Cohen are assumed to be descendants of the priestly class that served the Temple in biblical times, and under Jewish law priests are forbidden to marry converts or widows. He appealed to the Philadelphia congregation for permission to marry the widow Mordecai. After heated debate, the *junta* of Congregation Mikveh Israel ordered its minister, Gershom Mendes Seixas, not to perform the ceremony, and, in fact, not even to mention the couple's names within the synagogue. Not to be denied, Esther and Jacob found a learned Jewish layman who agreed to marry them. Later, after Esther's death, Jacob Cohen left Richmond and returned to Philadelphia, where he became president of Mikveh Israel.

No story of the Jewish experience in Virginia would be complete without reference to the Sage of Monticello, Thomas Jefferson. The liberties enjoyed by all religious bodies in the Old Dominion trace directly to Jefferson's Statute for Religious Freedom, but the connection between Jews and Jefferson extended far beyond that epochal document.

In Charlottesville, David Isaacs owned a dry goods store on Main Street, and it is said that he sold Jefferson the ball of twine that the latter used to lay out Pavilion VII, the first building of what would be the University of Virginia. In addition to providing Jefferson with meat, butter, cheese, and other items, Isaacs also undertook to furnish Jefferson with books and pamphlets on Judaism.

When Jefferson came to found the university, his plan included the then radical notion that there should be no sectarian religious studies required of the students, at a time when students in American colleges not only had to take such courses but also had to attend chapel on a regular basis. Jefferson's desire to make the university a true center of intellectual inquiry, and not a home for denominational indoctrination, can be seen in a letter he wrote to Isaac Harby in 1826: "I have thought it a cruel addition to the wrongs which that injured sect [Jews] have suffered that their youths should be excluded from the instructions in science afforded to all others in our public seminaries by imposing on them a course of theological reading which their consciences do not permit them to pursue, and in the University lately established here we have set the example of ceasing to violate the rights of conscience by any injunctions on the different sects respecting their religion."

In 1841 the University of Virginia announced two appointments: the twenty-six-year-old James Joseph Sylvester of England to teach mathematics and Charles Kraitsir of Hungary to teach modern languages. Kraitsir was a Catholic and Sylvester a Jew, the first Jew, in fact, hired to teach a secular subject in any American university. Jefferson would have been pleased by the appointment but angry not only at the treatment Sylvester received but also at the conditions that had befallen his "academical village."

The preceding year had been a low point in the university's short history. Violence among students escalated into the shooting of the chairman of the faculty. The professors then voted to arm themselves, which did little to calm the inflamed atmosphere. In this environment Sylvester arrived and initially received a hearty welcome from the university community, a popularity that increased once it became clear that he was a gifted teacher. Unfortunately, not all Virginians welcomed the appointment. The *Watchman of the South*, the Richmond-based organ of the Presbyterian church, wrote a vehemently anti-Semitic editorial attacking the appointments of Sylvester and Kraitsir and declaring that "public sentiment in Virginia will not sustain such a procedure. . . . We have often said that as infidelity became ashamed of its own colors, it would seek to form alliances with Papism, Unitarianism, Judaism, and other errors subversive of Christianity."

Only four months after his arrival in Charlottesville, Sylvester was confronted by a pupil and forced to defend himself with his sword cane.

Although authorities eventually expelled the culprit, the student's friends continued to harass Sylvester, and neither the faculty nor the board rallied to his defense as he thought they should. The following March, Sylvester left Virginia. His distinguished career took him to posts in both the United States and England. He became one of the first Jews to be appointed to Oxford after that university abolished its religious tests in 1871.

Jefferson had been dead fifteen years by the time Sylvester arrived in Charlottesville. Chronically in debt throughout his life, the Sage of Monticello had died owing large sums of money. He bequeathed his plantation to his one surviving child, Martha Jefferson Randolph, who upon the death of her husband in 1828 put the estate up for sale. In 1831 an eccentric Charlottesville chemist and preacher, James T. Barclay, bought Monticello for $7,000, and when his dream of turning it into a mulberry plantation to raise silkworms failed, he allowed the building and grounds to lapse into decay.

In the meantime, Commodore Uriah P. Levy, the man who abolished flogging in the United States Navy, became interested in Monticello.

Watchman of the South

Richmond, Thursday, August 5, 1841

They (the Board of Visitors) met and gave one vacant professorship to a Jew of London and another to a Hungarian Papist. This is the heaviest blow the University has ever received. Some things clergymen have not a good opportunity of learning...but we are not deceived in saying that public sentiment in Virginia will not sustain such a procedure. It was wholly unnecessary. We are informed on what we regard as good authority, that there were more than thirty candidates for one of these vacancies, and more than forty for the other. Among them were some of the most gifted and cultivated minds in our country, minds too adorned with Christian virtues and Christian principles...

We have often said that as infidelity became ashamed of its own colors, it would seek to form alliances with Papism, Unitarianism, Judaism, and other errors subversive of Christianity.

Albemarle Historical Society

The *Watchman of the South*, the Richmond-based newspaper of the Presbyterian church, protested the University of Virginia's hiring of James Joseph Sylvester as professor of mathematics in 1841.

Commodore Uriah P. Levy purchased Monticello in 1836 for $2,700. He and his nephew, Jefferson Levy, preserved and restored the estate, and in 1923 the Thomas Jefferson Memorial Foundation acquired the house and land for $500,000.

Jefferson had been his boyhood hero, and while in France Levy had met the aging marquis de Lafayette, who had asked what had become of his friend Jefferson's wonderful home. Levy promised to investigate and in the spring of 1836 made his first visit up the "little mountain." What he saw appalled him—218 acres of overgrown fields around a once great house falling into ruin. Levy purchased the estate for $2,700 and began what he hoped would be the restoration of the property. He bought up some of the surrounding land so that within a few years the estate had grown to 2,700 acres, and Levy himself often guided the groups of visitors who had begun to seek out Jefferson's home.

Levy last visited Monticello in 1860 and died in New York two years later. The complicated provisions of his elaborate will would have been difficult to execute even if the Civil War had not intervened. After hostilities had ended, his nephew, Jefferson Levy, persuaded the other heirs to sell their interests to him, and he became the sole owner in 1879. The true restoration of Monticello dates from that time. Jefferson Levy hired Thomas L. Rhodes to work with him

Jefferson Monroe Levy (1852–1924), a New York attorney, inherited Monticello from his uncle and began renovating the structure and reassembling objects that had belonged to the third president. Levy served as a Democrat in the Fifty-sixth, Sixty-second, and Sixty-third congresses.

Virginia Historical Society

on renovating the building; they also purchased Jefferson furniture when they could find it or had reproductions made.

Levy, who served as a congressman from 1899 to 1901 and then again from 1911 to 1915, earned his living as an attorney in New York and used that income to help rebuild Monticello. In the financial depression following World War I, he found he could no longer afford to keep the property and offered the federal government the opportunity to purchase it, an offer Congress debated extensively but eventually declined. In 1923 a group of public-spirited citizens formed the Thomas Jefferson Memorial Foundation, which purchased Monticello from Levy for $500,000. The work of the foundation in preserving Monticello as one of the nation's great historical sites is well known, but had it not been for Uriah Levy and his nephew, Monticello would have fallen into ruin many years before. Rachel Phillips Levy, Uriah's mother, is buried there; her once neglected grave has been

refurbished and an interpretive sign placed there in a rededication ceremony in 1985 so that visitors can learn about the role the Levy family played
in saving Jefferson's home.

Life was good for the Jews of Virginia in these early years of the new
republic. The equality promised in the Virginia statute and in the First
Amendment appears to have translated into reality. Jews served as
members of the Richmond city council, Joseph Darmstadt and Benjamin
Wolfe in the early nineteenth century, Solomon Jacobs as acting mayor of
the city in 1815. Gustavus A. Myers assumed a vacant council seat in 1827
and was then reelected twenty-six consecutive times. During twelve of his
nearly thirty years of service, Myers headed the city council, and among his
other civic endeavors, he helped to found the Virginia Historical Society in
1831. In 1807 Governor James Monroe named Jacob I. Cohen, one of the
founders of Beth Shalome, as an inspector of the state penitentiary. Jews
could also be found as members of the prestigious Richmond Light Infantry
Blues. Privates Tobias Ezekiel, David Judah, Manual Judah, and Moses H.
Judah and Corporal Zalma Rehiné saw three weeks of active service in July
1807, after the Blues were ordered to Portsmouth to counter threats of a
British landing following the *Chesapeake-Leopard* affair. Richmond Jews
continued to be active in the Blues throughout the early republic and
antebellum period.

In Norfolk, Moses Myers played an important role in the development
of that city's port. After the failure of his business in 1819, Myers applied
to the administration of President James Monroe for the position of
collector of customs in Norfolk. The request was transmitted by his son,
John Myers, whom Monroe had known because of John's service as
aide-de-camp to General Winfield Scott at Norfolk during the War of 1812.
Two petitions supported his suit, one signed by forty-nine merchants of the
town, including several Jews, and the other by eighty-seven citizens of
Norfolk, not one of whom was Jewish. All the signatures for both petitions
had been gathered on a single day, indicating the high esteem Myers
enjoyed among his fellow citizens. Monroe named Myers to the post, and
he proved to be an honest and efficient public servant.

In 1829, as a result of the reshuffling of patronage positions following
the election of Andrew Jackson, an effort to oust Myers nearly succeeded.
A petition to Jackson, signed by 227 Norfolk merchants (only one of whom
can positively be identified as Jewish) attesting to Myers's integrity and the
respect he commanded in the commercial community, led Old Hickory to
reappoint him.

American Jewish Historical Society, Waltham, Massachusetts

In April 1807, Jacob I. Cohen received an appointment from Governor James Monroe as inspector of the state penitentiary.

If individual Jews prospered and found themselves well accepted into the larger society, however, Jewish life itself remained precarious outside Richmond, where Beth Shalome served as an anchor to communal life.

The joys of living in a nation free of anti-Semitism, as well as the difficulties in remaining Jewish, are captured in two remarkable letters written by Rebecca Samuel of Petersburg in the early 1790s to her parents

Richea Myers (1769–1837), a daughter of New York goldsmith Myer Myers, married Joseph Marx, a recent German immigrant, and moved to Richmond. In this portrait by John Wesley Jarvis, she wears a *sheitel* (false curls) under her turban.

Valentine Museum, Richmond

in Europe. Hyman Samuel, a watchmaker and silversmith, lived in Petersburg in the early 1790s, and his wife talked candidly about the difficulties of maintaining Jewish practice. In a letter dated 12 January 1791, she complained that "when the Jews of Philadelphia or New York hear the name Virginia, they get nasty. And they are not wrong! It won't do for a Jew. In the first place it is an unhealthful district, and we are only human. God forbid, if anything should happen to us, where would we be thrown? There is no [Jewish] cemetery in the whole of Virginia." (The Beth Shalome cemetery was established later that year.)

Yet she had to admit that "one can make a good living here, and all live at peace. Anyone can do what he wants. There is no rabbi in all of America to excommunicate anyone. This is a blessing here; Jew and Gentile are as one. There is no [rejection of Jews] here."

In a second, undated letter, Samuel informed her parents that she and her family were leaving Petersburg for Charleston, South Carolina, which had an established Jewish community and a synagogue. "The whole reason we are leaving this place is because of the lack of Jewishness," she wrote. "Dear parents, I know quite well you will not want me to bring up my children like Gentiles. Here they cannot be anything else. Jewishness is pushed aside here. There are here ten or twelve Jews, and they are not worthy of being called Jews." She went on to lament the absence of a synagogue and the other communal agencies that would support Jewish life, but once again she reassured her parents that life in America posed no threats from hostility on the part of their Christian neighbors. Nor did Jews lack economic opportunity in Petersburg. She reported that her husband's watch-making business had prospered. The Samuels moved to Charleston and then in 1796 settled in Richmond, where Rebecca and their children could enjoy the benefits of a more substantial community.

Although there were enough Jews in Petersburg for the ritual *minyan* in the 1790s, a synagogue was not established for several more decades. Nonetheless, Petersburg Jews—as Rebecca Samuel noted—enjoyed cordial relations with their Christian neighbors, and one wrote that even though they had no synagogue, "it is believed that we will be fully aided by Christian friends in building one." By the 1820s, a learned immigrant from Augsburg, Germany, one Adam S. Naustedler, had arrived in the city. While supporting himself through a business, Naustedler, whom a contemporary noted was "profoundly versed in the Talmud and in [Jewish] traditions," officiated when Petersburg Jews gathered for prayer. He was apparently often called "rabbi."

The problems of living Jewishly were not unique to Jews in the Virginia of the early republic; they were, and are, common in all societies in which Jews have enjoyed the blessings of liberty. The existence of an organized community makes it easier to fulfill the commandments of the faith, but it does not remove the centrifugal forces that liberty exerts on self-contained groups. In Europe, several pressures forced Jews to remain Jewish. The anti-Semitic laws of many countries gave Jews only two options—to reside within the Jewish community or to convert to Christianity and give up Judaism completely. If they chose to remain Jewish, the leaders of the community were able to employ a variety of pressures to make individuals conform to both religious and secular standards of behavior. The "wall of Torah" that helped preserve Jews against outer tyranny also locked them into a closed community that offered few choices other than strict adherence to the faith.

In every open society in which Jews have lived, these centripetal pressures have dissipated. The choice was no longer between living as the community decreed or abandoning Judaism. One could live as a Jew, even outside the communal structure. Just as the Puritans discovered that freedom broke down the safeguards they tried to build around their piety, so, too, the Jewish communities of the New World found that liberty exerted a great pull. Jews who wanted to remain Jewish could do so without fear of persecution. Other Jews, for whatever reason, chose to assimilate and to marry outside the faith; their children, and almost certainly their

Gustavus Adolphus Myers (1801–1869), shown here in a painting by Thomas Sully, was a founder of the Virginia Historical Society and twice acted as master of his Masonic lodge. For thirty years he sat on Richmond's city council and served as its president 1843–55.

Virginia Historical Society

grandchildren, more often than not grew up as Christians. Intermarriage, dangerous as it was and is to Jewish survival, is also testimony to the true openness of American society. In Europe, laws prohibited Jews and Christians from marrying; in America, the promise of religious freedom removed a person's faith as an issue in the eyes of the law and also in terms of potential marriage partners.

Gustavus Myers, who served so long as a pillar of the Richmond Jewish and civil communities, married Anne Giles Conway, the widowed daughter of Governor William Branch Giles, an Episcopalian. Nearly all of the First Jewish Families of Virginia left the Jewish community through intermarriage and assimilation within three generations. They could withstand the calls of missionaries to convert but not the promise of full acceptance into the wider community. The names of many of these families are still extant in Virginia, but their bearers no longer practice Judaism and in some instances have not done so for several generations. As one newspaperman noted recently, there are many Christian families who have, both literally and figuratively, a menorah in the attic.

Had the Jewish communities of Virginia been dependent on these early settlers remaining Jewish, it is unlikely that they would have survived long into the nineteenth century. But growth did occur, some by natural increase and some by immigration. The census of 1820 counted some three hundred Jews in the Old Dominion, and two hundred of them lived in Richmond. By that year, Richmond had a total population greater than 12,000, and the members of Beth Shalome decided that they could afford a permanent house of worship.

As the congregation had grown, it had moved its meeting place from rented rooms on Nineteenth Street to a small brick building on the southwestern corner of Nineteenth and Main, in the rear of what was then known as the Union Hotel. The spiritual leader of Beth Shalome at the time was a man described by one historian as "the most learned of American Jews in the early 19th century," Israel Baer Kursheedt. Born near Frankfurt in 1766, he arrived in New York in 1796, where he found economic conditions so far from conducive to earning a livelihood that in 1812 he moved to Richmond. Though his family traveled overland by stagecoach, he sent his extensive Hebrew library and his Masonic materials by ship. The United States had just declared war on Great Britain, and an enemy frigate captured the vessel carrying Kursheedt's belongings. A number of years later, a boat arrived in Richmond with his trunks, and Kursheedt always believed the return of his cherished possessions was the gesture of a fellow Mason, though whether Jewish or Christian he did not know.

Kursheedt stayed in the Virginia capital for twelve years. During that time he helped to reorganize the congregation and led its members to undertake the building of a permanent synagogue. As was so often the case in these years, older and more established congregations gave gifts to smaller groups to enable them to purchase land or erect buildings. In 1809 Shearith Israel, the great Sephardic congregation of New York, sent Beth Shalome a gift of $360 to be used for a new synagogue. (The figure is twenty times *chai*, the Hebrew word that means "life" and whose letters have a numerical value of eighteen.) In 1818 Beth Shalome purchased a lot on the east side of Mayo Street just north of Franklin, in what was then considered the most desirable residential district in the city. In March 1822, the congregation issued an appeal for funds. Sufficient money came in to erect a handsome building in time for High Holiday services that fall. On 15 September 1822, Beth Shalome consecrated the first synagogue building in Virginia, where the congregation worshiped for the next sixty-nine years. In 1891 the new Russian congregation, Sir Moses Montefiore, purchased the structure, which at that time was the third oldest synagogue building in the United States.

By the early 1840s, Jews could be found in Petersburg, Charlottesville, Norfolk, and other towns in the state, but the largest number resided in

Educator and author Jacob Mordecai delivered a discourse at the consecration of Beth Shalome in Richmond.

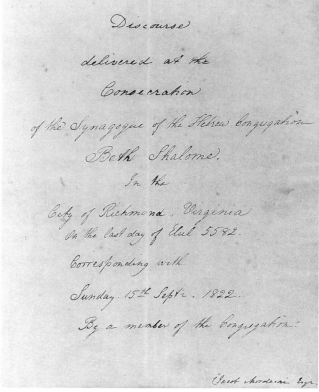

Discourse delivered at the Consecration of the Synagogue of the Hebrew Congregation Beth Shalome. In the City of Richmond, Virginia On the last day of Elul 5582. Corresponding with Sunday. 15th Septr. 1822. By a member of the Congregation.

American Jewish Historical Society, Waltham, Massachusetts

Richmond. The community there had grown and prospered for several reasons. As the capital of the state, Richmond provided economic opportunity that laid the financial basis for the growth of Beth Shalome. The religious freedom promised in the statute of 1786 had indeed materialized, and Jews appeared to enjoy a real social and political equality within the city. One measure of how seriously they took that equality, and how rigorously they exercised their freedom, can be seen in the community's response to anti-Semitism abroad and at home.

An especially virulent anti-Semitic episode that occurred in 1840, the so-called Damascus affair, served to underline the freedom that the Jews of Virginia and of the United States enjoyed. In that year a monk, Father Thomas, and his assistant mysteriously disappeared in Damascus, and thirteen Jews of that city were seized by the authorities, tortured, and charged with the murder of Father Thomas for the purpose of using his blood for religious rituals. Jewish communities throughout western Europe and the United States protested and called on their governments to act. The politics of the Middle East and imperial ambitions there made it difficult for European governments to do anything, even though their leaders considered the blood libel ridiculous and the actions of the viceroy of Egypt, who then controlled Damascus, to be reprehensible. Such considerations did not affect the United States. When the congregations of New York and Richmond appealed to President Martin Van Buren, the American government instructed its consul in Egypt, John Glidden, to make known to the Egyptian authorities its abhorrence of their conduct in Damascus. In addition, the State Department urged Glidden to do whatever he could to relieve the distress of the victims.

In September the officials of Beth Shalome wrote to the president to express their gratitude for his actions. In words that echoed the letter to George Washington a half century earlier, the Jews of Richmond thanked Van Buren and also noted "the civil and religious privileges secured to us by the Constitution of this favored land."

The response to local slurs on Jews came from a young member of the community, Isaac Leeser. Born in Westphalia in 1806, Leeser graduated from a secular gymnasium and also studied the Talmud. He then emigrated to America at age seventeen to work in the Richmond store of his uncle, Zalma Rehiné. There he found ample time to indulge in his voracious reading habits as well as to assist the lector at Beth Shalome's services. In late 1828 a New York paper reprinted a series of anti-Semitic articles that

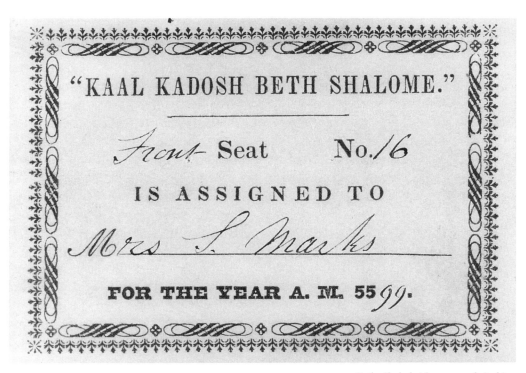

Beth Ahabah Museum and Archives

Beth Shalome in Richmond assigned seating for the High Holidays in 1839.

Isaac Leeser (1806–1868), founder of the Jewish press in America, arrived in Richmond in 1824. After his newspaper articles in defense of Jews attracted widespread attention, he moved to Philadelphia and established *The Occident and American Jewish Advocate*.

Maxwell Whiteman Collection; photograph courtesy of the Valentine Museum, Richmond

had originally appeared in the *London Quarterly Review*. The articles incensed Leeser, and he immediately sat down to write a response, thus launching himself on what would turn out to be his life's work, journalism and education. The six essays he wrote appeared in the *Richmond Whig*, edited by one of the luminaries of Virginia journalism, John Hampden Pleasants. Not only did Pleasants open his paper to Leeser, but he also drew attention to the series by publishing an editorial commending the young writer and condemning attacks on Jews. The fame garnered by these articles, as well as by a book on Mosaic law he wrote while in Richmond, gained Leeser national acclaim, and in 1829, despite his lack of rabbinical training, the prestigious Congregation Mikveh Israel called Leeser to Philadelphia to be its spiritual leader.

Even as Virginia Jewry rejoiced in this latest proof that Jews truly enjoyed freedom in this "second Jerusalem," events in Europe transformed the nature of the American Jewish community in general and that of Virginia in particular. The great migration of German Jews to the New World had begun.

THE ARRIVAL OF THE GERMANS

THE story has been told in the family for several generations, and although largely apocryphal, it has some element of truth. Four young men left their homes in central Europe in 1840 to come to the New World to seek a better life, greater economic opportunity, and religious freedom. They made their way to Le Havre, France, where they met on board a steamer bound for New Orleans. Once in America, they supposedly traveled up and down the Mississippi for a while, peddling household goods, and then they headed north toward Pittsburgh.

Only one of them, Edger Kaufman, actually reached Pittsburgh. Lewis Rosenstock stopped in Petersburg and because of his poor grasp of English mistook Petersburg for Pittsburgh. In any event, so the story goes, he liked the small southern town and opened a store there that bore his name for the next century. Lewis Stern, the third of the travelers, went on to New York, where he founded Stern Brothers, one of that city's great department stores. The fourth seeker, William (Wolf) Thalheimer, came to Richmond, where he met and married Mary Millhiser, another German immigrant. In 1842 he, too, opened a department store, one that became not only the largest in Richmond but in later years would have branches in other parts of the state as well.

Not all German Jewish immigrants to the United States in the mid-nineteenth century founded department stores, but it is amazing how many of the great mercantile houses of this country owe their origins to that group, including Filene's in Boston; Lazarus in Ohio; Macy's, Abraham & Straus, Gimbels, and Stern Brothers in New York; Rich's in Atlanta; and Nieman-Marcus in Dallas. If ever a time and a place and a people came together successfully, it would be hard to find a better example than the Jews who came to the United States from central Europe starting in the late 1820s. They transformed the Jewish landscape of the country in general, and of Virginia as well.

The conditions of Jews in the German states in the early nineteenth century made these people ripe for emigration to the New World. Mainly artisans and small merchants, they labored under heavy taxes and humiliating restrictions that subverted any chance of either business success or

As Kathie Hofmayer prepared to emigrate from Bavaria, she had this ruby-and-crystal mug etched with scenes of her homeland. After her arrival in America, she married William Fleishman of Richmond.

Beth Ahabah Museum and Archives

personal fulfillment. Bavaria, for example, limited the number of Jewish marriages. The emancipation of Jews begun under Napoleon had barely filtered into central Europe when the French emperor fell, and it was several decades before Jews broke free of anti-Semitic regulations. A severe economic depression led many to seek a better life across the Atlantic, and a steady flow of Jews from the German states, Austria, Bohemia, Hungary, and western Poland—all of whom spoke German and shared German cultural values—moved westward to America. Between 1840 and 1880, nearly 200,000 of them came, overwhelming the earlier, predominantly Sephardic community, which numbered about 15,000 in 1840. Where there had been only six Jewish congregations established in the eighteenth century, by 1850 eighty-five congregations could be counted in forty-eight cities, and the nuclei of Jewish communities could be found in at least fifty additional locations. Nearly all this growth can be attributed to the German migration.

The newcomers amazed the Sephardim, not only because of their poverty, but also because they were a different type of Jew. In northern Europe, Jews followed the Ashkenazic rituals and spoke Hebrew with a

In 1857 Lewis and Rosalie Hutzler Held posed for an ambrotype with their children, Amelia, Fanny, Mathilda, and Isaac. Held ran a dry goods store in Richmond.

Beth Ahabah Museum and Archives

more guttural, German accent. Because many of them had been traders in Europe, they strapped on packs and fanned out across the country. They went west or south, lugging on their backs the goods needed by a frontier society—needles, thread, pots and pans, ribbons and tools. In the cities as well Jewish peddlers went from door to door selling clothes, food, and household utensils.

The newcomers brought with them a strong sense of religion, because in the world they had left behind, the only sure protection they had been able to rely on was within the Jewish community. Even those who did not have deeply felt religious beliefs nonetheless had strong ties to their fellow Jews. One of the peddlers who came through and stayed in Richmond during this period, Herman Kahn (who later, as Herman Cone, established the Cone Mills in North Carolina), carried in his baggage a letter he and his descendants treasured. It had been written by his brother-in-law, Joseph Rosengart, and it reflected both the hopes that Jews had for themselves in America and the hope they had for Judaism in this new country. A portion of this letter sums up the sentiments that many of the German Jews had when they came to their new homes:

> You may shed tears, because you are leaving your parents' house, your father, brothers, and sisters, relatives, friends, and your native land, but dry your tears, because you may have the sweet hope of finding a second home abroad and a new

country where you will not be deprived of all political and civil rights and where the Jew is not excluded from the society of all other men and subject to the severest restrictions, but you will find a real homeland where you as a human being may claim all human rights and human dignity. . . .

I recommend to you the faith of your fathers as the most sacred and the most noble. Try to follow all the Commandments most painstakingly and thereby attain actual happiness. Do not sacrifice your faith for worldly goods. They will disappear like dust and must be left behind in due time. . . .

I am, therefore, giving you as a keepsake an excellent religious book for your instruction. Make it your sacred duty to read one chapter on each Sabbath and holy day with serious devotion and meditation. Do not lay it aside when you have read it through, but keep it and read it again from time to time. You will thereby learn your religion thoroughly, act accordingly, and thus be honored by God and men. It will be your counsel in good times and bad and will preserve you from all evil.

As a group, the Germans proved enormously influential in American Jewish development. They brought with them the ideas of Reform Judaism, which they helped to establish in the United States. The Reform movement held, among other things, that modern Jews should abandon any desire to return to live in Palestine but should instead make Jewish lives for themselves wherever they lived; that the rituals and prayer books should be updated to reflect modern ideas; that sermons should be delivered in the vernacular; that men and women should not be separated during services; and that music, including the use of organs and choirs, would enhance the beauty as well as the decorum of services. Although these matters may seem commonplace at the end of the twentieth century, in the middle of the nineteenth they created an uproar in Jewish communities in both America and Germany and often led to congregations splitting apart over the issue of whether to adopt the reforms or adhere to traditional beliefs and practices.

The Germans also created many of the great communal institutions that looked after the welfare of the community. On the local level, they established hospitals and social service agencies in each community with a significant Jewish population. On the national scene, the first generation of German Jews set up B'nai Brith, the Union of American Hebrew Congregations, the American Jewish Committee, and both the Hebrew Union College to train Reform rabbis and the Jewish Theological Seminary to train Conservative leaders.

In Virginia, the transformation wrought by the newcomers echoed what took place on the national scale. Virginia Jewry in the 1820s consisted of a fair-sized community in Richmond and smaller groupings in Petersburg, Tidewater, and the western part of the state, totaling perhaps 400 persons. The only synagogue was Beth Shalome in Richmond. By 1880, the Jewish population in the Old Dominion had grown to 2,600, with synagogues in several cities.

Beth Ahabah Museum and Archives

Charles Mitteldorfer of Richmond wore this handworked gown at his circumcision ceremony in 1840.

Although the numbers may not look large, the energy and the tenacity of this wave of migration left a permanent mark wherever it washed ashore. In Richmond, Norfolk, and other parts of the state, a number of today's communal organizations and synagogues owe their origins and much of their vitality to the newcomers who arrived in this period.

One might ask why so few actually came to Virginia. Only a little more than 1 percent of the 200,000 who migrated to the United States between 1840 and 1880 chose to settle in the Old Dominion. There are several answers to this question. First and foremost, the greatest economic growth, and therefore the greatest opportunities for newcomers, could be found north of Mason and Dixon's line. Second, in the northern states newcomers found most of the established Jewish communities of the time. Finally, for new immigrants, many of whom had no capital and saw manual labor as their starting point in the New World, a rural agrarian society based on slave labor offered few attractions.

The ones who did settle, especially in the earlier years, may have responded to the fact that German-speaking communities already existed in parts of Virginia. Richmond, which continued throughout this period as the largest Jewish community in the state, had an extensive German presence, about one-fourth of the white population. Germans had also established themselves in the Shenandoah Valley and in both instances appeared to have welcomed those who came from German-speaking central Europe, whatever their religion happened to be.

In looking at the years before the Civil War (and in some cases afterward as well), a clear pattern emerges. The older communities had begun to stagnate, losing members through death, departure, or intermarriage. The newcomers invigorated the communities, established businesses, some of which proved quite successful, and then organized charitable agencies and especially synagogues, many of which are still in existence. It is the synagogue that in some ways is most important, because it provided the anchor for the community, a place of worship and learning, and the means by which its members could more easily lead Jewish lives.

In Virginia as elsewhere, many of the newcomers initially supported themselves as peddlers. Those with the least amount of capital carried their goods in a backpack; those who did well and accumulated some money graduated to a cart and one or two horses. They peddled their goods in the towns and villages and in the countryside, and by the 1850s, the number of peddlers, both Jewish and non-Jewish, had increased to the point that local citizens often complained and the General Assembly felt it necessary to impose some control on the traffic.

In February 1841, for example, John Smith of Loudoun County wrote to his representative, Sanford J. Ramey, that "during the present winter, this part of the county has been inundated by . . . Foreign pedlars to the great detriment of the regular Merchants whose sales have been considerably curtailed." The following winter merchants in the area signed a petition to the assembly complaining that "much injury is sustained annually by the public . . . in consequence of hawkers and pedlars not naturalized and other hawkers and pedlars. . . . [They] come into the county of Loudo[u]n with their merchandise and fraudulently impose their articles upon the citizens. They then disappear and are succeeded by others who assume the right to trade under the license which their predecessors traded under claiming to belong to a firm."

The legislature had, in fact, been trying to regulate peddlers ever since 1738, when it imposed a fifteen-shilling license fee and a £20 bond. In 1814, as part of the general taxation scheme, the assembly initiated a license fee for store owners and peddlers of non-Virginia-made dry goods, clocks, tin, and pewter ware. Although the complaints did not specifically mention Jews but referred instead to "foreigners," there can be little doubt that many of these peddlers were Jewish. The 1850 census of Virginia listed many peddlers, including Hyman Levy (Louisa County), Isaac Solomon (Richmond), Moses Einstein (Montgomery County), Joel Goodman (Essex County), Absalom Hech (Giles County), Charles Held (Richmond), Abraham Orberndoffer (Cumberland County), and Jacob Meyer (Hanover County).

German Jewish peddlers could be found in all parts of the state, and if their travel patterns were anything like their brethren in Europe, it is likely that many of them knew each other or their families. When Jews traveled, they often stayed with other Jews, partly out of fear of anti-Semitism, but also because they felt more comfortable in a Jewish household, especially one where they could speak German. Moreover, a Jew who kept the Sabbath might not always be able to get back home by Friday evening, and so he would seek out a Jewish household where he could partake of the Sabbath meal and ritual and, if there was a *minyan* or a synagogue in that town, join other Jews in their weekly devotions.

William Thalhimer, like many of his fellow immigrants, started out as a peddler. He drove a horse and cart through Richmond's East End and sold household goods to the residents, before he accumulated enough money to open a store. In today's parlance, he and his wife ran a "mom-and-pop" operation in an eighteen-by-sixty-foot room on the lower floor of a building on Main Street between Seventeenth and Eighteenth streets, near what was then the heart of Richmond's business district. Mary Thalhimer played an important role in the business and seems to have been responsible for much of the buying of goods. An important contribution to the store's success derived from William Thalhimer's innovative pricing policy. Rather than haggling over what prices should be, he set one price on an item that did not vary on a daily basis. Moreover, he established a liberal return policy, so

The kiddush, a prayer over the wine, is performed in observing the Jewish Sabbath and festivals. This coin silver kiddush cup was "Presented by the Hebrews of Norfolk Va. To Rev'd M. J. Michelbacher" of Richmond in 1853.

that if customers did not find the goods satisfactory, they could return them. Within a few years the store had prospered to the point that the Thalhimers needed additional space, and they moved to larger quarters on the same street.

German immigrants opened other businesses in Richmond, such as William Flegenheimer's Southern Commercial College on Main Street. City records in 1852 list more than twenty-five German Jewish merchants in the dry goods business, while others owned butcher shops, jewelry stores, tailor shops, and confectioneries.

One of the great success stories is that of Samuel Binswanger, who in 1872 founded the glass company that still bears his name. The firm began as a small retail glass store, selling items in a city trying to rebuild itself, literally, from the ashes of the Civil War. Soon, in addition to his store, Binswanger had a mule-drawn cart that allowed him and his sons to expand their sales territory. The sons, Harry and Moses, did much of the traveling while their father oversaw the store and took care of securing the glass for which there seemed a constantly growing demand. Eventually all four of Samuel's sons joined the business, which grew from a store to a large warehouse to an industrial plant serving several states.

The Richmond congregation, Beth Shalome, even though it had originally included Jews from Germany and Poland, had adopted the Sephardic ritual and, like the other established communities of the time (with whom it kept up close contact), was relatively prosperous but parochial; it nervously welcomed the newcomers but was unsure of what to make of them. The newcomers initially joined Beth Shalome, but as their numbers grew, they found themselves uncomfortable.

In 1839 they established Chebrah Ahabat Israel, the Association for the Love of Israel, a social as well as a philanthropic society. Two years later, under the leadership of Myer Angle, the Germans organized K'hal Kadosh Beth Ahabah—the Holy Congregation House of Love. Although Beth Ahabah became one of the preeminent Reform congregations of the country, at the time of its founding the German Jews did not want to institute reform so much as to get away from the Sephardic ritual and to pray in the Ashkenazic fashion to which they had been accustomed in the Old Country.

Initially Beth Ahabah met in rented rooms, but the financial success of its members allowed it to hire a full-time spiritual leader within five years. The arrival of Maximilian J. Michelbacher from Philadelphia served as a catalyst to the growth of the new congregation. Michelbacher was not an ordained rabbi but a teacher and a reader, that is, one familiar with Hebrew who could read the Torah and conduct the services. Upon his arrival he established the Richmond German, Hebrew, and English Institute and by September 1847 had enrolled seventy pupils. The school provided secular

Although Maximilian J. Michelbacher (1810–1879) never received rabbinic ordination, he led Congregation Beth Ahabah in Richmond with distinction for more than thirty years.

Cook Collection, Valentine Museum, Richmond

education during the week and religious instruction on Saturdays. (At this time there were no public schools in Richmond or, for that matter, in most of the southern states.)

Michelbacher also spurred the building of a permanent synagogue. A small group met at his home in February 1847 and formed a building committee. On 27 July of that year, they issued a call for funds and quickly raised nearly $2,900, of which $810 came from their Christian neighbors. The new synagogue, the first permanent home of Beth Ahabah, was built on Eleventh Street between Marshall and Clay, and the congregation moved in following dedicatory services led by Michelbacher on 22 September 1848. According to one witness, the ceremony was all in Hebrew except for Michelbacher's sermon, but even that could barely be understood by some as he "speaks very bad English yet awhile." By 1851, the original membership of forty had more than doubled, and the student enrollment at Michelbacher's school had tripled. Beth Ahabah was easily outstripping Beth Shalome as the leading congregation in the city.

The vitality of the German Jews in Richmond matched that of their compatriots elsewhere, not only in establishing synagogues but also in their cultural and intellectual life. As Michael A. Meyer has noted, many of the German immigrants had little time in the beginning for either religion or culture, but as they settled and prospered, they devoted their efforts to both. In Richmond the school and other activities that Maximilian Michelbacher established primarily served children, but they also engaged in what we would now call "adult education."

Both men and women formed literary clubs, in which they read books and debated questions of the day. The oldest of the Richmond men's clubs, the Old Dominion Debating Society, first met on 31 August 1856 and included most of the leaders of Beth Ahabah as well as its spiritual leader. A Jefferson Literary Association came into being in 1867, and according to Charles Hutzler, the members would debate anything. "In those days," he wrote, "if we had an argument or debate upon any subject, as for instance: whether the turkey-gobbler was justifiable in picking the grasshopper off the sweet potato vine, the appointees would prepare themselves by reading Blackstone, Tucker, Grattan and English History with the same degree of interest as if they were engaged to prosecute or defend a criminal on trial for the assassination of the Czar of All the Russias."

Women also formed clubs but at a later date. The elitist Progressive Literary Association began in 1888 and initially restricted itself to fifteen members, although a few years later it expanded to twenty women. Like the men, the women gathered both for social reasons and to engage in serious literary study. Minutes of the PLA show discussion topics to have included Greek, Roman, French, German, and Spanish history and literature, Milton, Browning, Tennyson, Byron, and Graetz's *History of the Jews*. Some societies merged with one another and some dissolved, but there are still remnants of them in Richmond today. The Old Dominion and Jefferson societies eventually evolved into the Jefferson-Lakeside Country Club,

Beth Ahabah Museum and Archives

Kenesseth Israel, Richmond's so-called Polish congregation, was established in 1856 by eastern Europeans and some Germans unhappy with the Reform efforts of Beth Ahabah. The Orthodox congregation used this brass menorah in the nineteenth century.

while the PLA continued to be active into the 1960s, when the women's movement and greater opportunities for women in higher education made the original need for the club superfluous. As You Like It, another women's group, remained active until 1984, when it voted to disband, while the Thirteen Class, founded in 1891, still meets regularly.

While the energy of Beth Shalome slowly seeped away and the vitality of the Germans and Beth Ahabah became the basis for Jewish life in

Richmond, a third group was equally unhappy with both congregations. The so-called Polish congregation, Kenesseth Israel (Congregation of Israel), was established in 1856 and included not only eastern Europeans but some Germans as well. As Beth Ahabah became more self-consciously Reform, and then in 1898 absorbed the remnants of Beth Shalome, Kenesseth Israel, later called Kenesseth Beth Israel, became for almost a century the Orthodox synagogue for Richmond Jews.

———

Similar stories can be told of other communities in Virginia. On the eve of the Civil War, the Petersburg city directory listed twenty-seven businesses owned by Jews, of which seventeen sold dry goods and nine others dealt with household items or clothing. In 1859 twenty-six-year-old Anthony Rosenstock (not the Lewis Rosenstock who supposedly came over nineteen years earlier with Wolf Thalheimer) opened a dry goods store that became the city's most important department store for the next hundred years. Rosenstock appears to have been an imaginative and aggressive advertiser. He called his store on Sycamore Street the Temple of Fancy. As his business prospered, he brought over three of his nephews, Isaac, Bernard, and Lewis Stern, who worked for him in his emporium for several years until they decided to go to New York, where they opened their own department store.

The various Jewish merchants in the city seemed to have kept the Sabbath fairly rigorously, and in 1859 the *Petersburg Daily Express* noted the closing of Jewish businesses on Saturday. "The members of the Israelitish congregation, residing in this city, have determined to observe Jewish Sabbath, which occurs to-day," the paper reported. "As many of the stores will be closed, those having business will be enabled to account for the temporary suspension. It is contemplated, we learn, to observe the day regularly in the future." By then, Petersburg had its first congregation, Rodef Shalom, organized on 15 August 1858, which worshiped in a building on Sycamore Street.

The birth of a congregation and the fact that Jewish merchants closed their shops on Saturday led Isaac Leeser, the noted editor of the *Occident and American Jewish Advocate*, to comment positively on Jewish life in the city when he visited there in May 1859. There were a number of Jews in Petersburg, most of them seemingly prosperous, and a benevolent aid society helped Jewish travelers and peddlers passing through the town. Nonetheless, a year later Leeser received a letter from a correspondent in Petersburg complaining about the poor quality of Jewish life there—the absence of a cemetery so that the dead had to be buried in Richmond, the dissolution of the charitable society, and other problems.

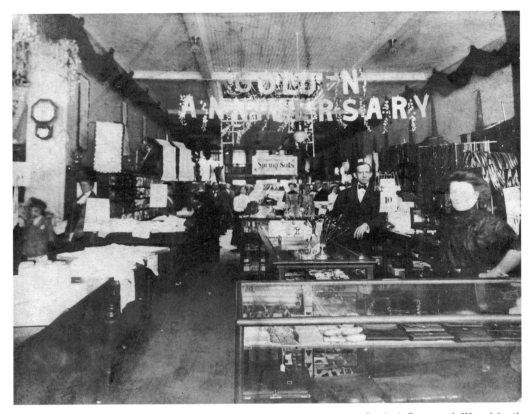

Louis A. Rosenstock III and family

German immigrant Anthony Rosenstock established a dry goods store he called the Temple of Fancy in Petersburg on the eve of the Civil War. A. Rosenstock & Co. celebrated its golden anniversary in 1909.

The main problem that faced not only Petersburg Jews but the entire city for the next few years was the Civil War and the devastation it wrought. Although the congregation had announced shortly after its formation that it would soon erect a synagogue, that dream had to be deferred for nearly two decades. After the war, Rodef Shalom hired a rabbi, M. J. Oppenheimer, who conducted services on the lower floor of the Masonic temple. Then in 1870 Rabbi Alexander Gross came to Petersburg, and during his tenure the congregation finally erected its sanctuary on Union Street in 1876.

In Charlottesville, three German Jewish families are credited with laying the foundations for the economic, civil, cultural, and religious life of the community. As one study of Charlottesville Jewry notes, these fami-

Isaac and Simon Leterman opened a retail store on Main Street in Charlottesville two years after their immigration from Württemberg. By the end of the nineteenth century, their mammoth building, shown on the left, contained nearly 50,000 square feet of floor space.

lies—the Letermans, the Oberdorfers, and the Kaufmans—"identified themselves as Virginians, businessmen, community leaders, and Jews. Their lives were embedded in the larger community; they were barely distinguishable by their religion."

Born in Württemberg in the 1820s, Isaac and Simon Leterman came to the United States with their wives and children about 1850, and in 1852 they opened a retail store on Main Street. Though kin and business partners, their political views took them in different directions in 1861. Isaac fought for the Union, and his younger brother Simon joined the Confederacy. Simon's wife, Hannah, volunteered as a nurse. After the war, there appear to have been several Leterman stores, the largest of which was owned by Simon's son Philip, whose father-in-law, Mayor Henry Strauss of Alexandria, had purchased a lot and helped him build a five-story building in 1889. A few years later, the four sons of Simon and Hannah combined their various ventures in Philip's building to create the largest store in Charlottesville.

Bernard Oberdorfer migrated from Württemberg to New York, where he worked in a cigar factory, and then moved to Charlottesville. He and his son Philip opened Oberdorfer & Son on Main Street, and like the

The Kaufmans were among the founding families of Charlottesville's Jewry. Kaufman's clothing store on Main Street, shown here in 1915, specialized in men's wear. Moses Kaufman also owned a whiskey warehouse and manufactured slate pencils and cigars.

Holsinger Studio Collection (#9862), Special Collections, Manuscript Division, University of Virginia Library

Letermans, they played a major role in the life of both the Jewish community and the larger society.

Isaac and Simon Leterman brought their nephew, Moses Kaufman, to the United States as an eleven-year-old in 1858; after the Civil War, he married Isaac Leterman's daughter Hannah. He, too, started a clothing store, right across the street from Oberdorfer's. The Kaufman store occupied the same site as had the first Jewish business in Charlottesville, the one owned by David Isaacs, and was in fact built by David's son, Tucker Isaacs. In addition to the clothing store, Moses Kaufman branched out into other activities. He owned a whiskey warehouse late in the nineteenth century and also manufactured slate pencils and cigars.

As Nancy Willner has noted, "a Jewish community is often dated from the establishment of its cemetery." Prayer services can be held anywhere, even in a private house, but a proper burial requires consecrated ground. A cemetery also implies permanence, a notice that symbolically, by burying its dead, the community is planting its roots. On 13 January 1870, Isaac Leterman and Bernard Oberdorfer purchased property on Cherry Street, next to the city's Oakwood Cemetery, and on the deed noted that they held the property "as trustees for the use and occupation and benefit of the

Hebrew congregation in Charlottesville." But as yet there was no formal congregation. A Hebrew Benevolent Society had been founded sometime in the 1860s to give aid to the needy and to provide for proper religious burial, and it was undoubtedly this society that had initiated the purchase of the burial ground. On 5 January 1882, the minutes of the last recorded meeting of that society noted that funds had been voted for a burial and to aid Russian refugees. By the next meeting, the Hebrew Benevolent Society had become the Beth Israel Congregation.

In early October 1882, the community gathered to lay the cornerstone for a synagogue, the first one west of Richmond, at the corner of Second and Market streets. The noted architect George W. Spooner had proposed a gothic revival design, one then popular for both churches and synagogues. As usual, the Masonic lodge, to which many of the city's Jews belonged, oversaw the ceremonies, which included a well-attended march down Main Street. Apparently non-Jews also helped in the construction, for at the dedication ceremony in June 1883, many Christians gathered with the congregation to celebrate the new synagogue. The president, D. H. Stern, offered "thanks to our Christian friends for their kindness and assistance in building this Temple," and he praised them for their financial as well as moral support.

Although Beth Israel immediately hired a rabbi, William Weinstein, the expenses proved too great for a community that numbered about one hundred. After a few years, the congregation adopted a policy of lay leadership, which remained in effect until the 1940s, when a Hillel chapter was established at the University of Virginia. From that time on, a rabbi has served jointly as chaplain of Hillel and spiritual leader of Beth Israel.

In 1904 the synagogue building was moved, brick by brick, to a new location at Third and Jefferson after the federal government sought the Second Street property on which to build a post office. The congregation split over the issue; the trustees voted to accept the $10,000 offered by the government. In Charlottesville city court, Moses Leterman sued the trustees on behalf of himself and other members of Beth Israel to stop the sale, and the trustees named as defendants in the case were his uncle, Isaac Leterman, and his father-in-law, Bernard Oberdorfer. The court ruled in favor of the trustees, who then in a gesture of peace named Moses Leterman head of the new building committee.

———

Sixty miles northwest of Charlottesville, over the Blue Ridge Mountains, lies Harrisonburg, where four Jewish families from Austria settled in 1859. Leopold Wise, Herman Heller, Samuel Loewner, Jonas Heller, and their families made their living not in dry goods but making combs from cow horns and buttons from bones and then peddling these items all over the state. Loewner, who had been a sculptor in Europe, also founded a marble business. He quarried native stone and made grave markers. Examples of his work can still be found in the older cemeteries in and around Harrisonburg. The success of these first four families led others from Germany and Bohemia to settle in the area.

The Civil War made a minor and temporary dent in the migrations from central Europe, but following Appomattox the number of immigrants rose sharply. Moreover, once the issue of slavery was resolved and German Jews well settled in Virginia, the state had attractions to the newcomers it lacked before the war. By 1867, the population of Harrisonburg had increased to the point that the Jewish families rented a room in the Paul building on West Market Street in which to hold services. Loewner, Wise, and a newcomer, Simon Oestreicher, conducted services according to traditional Orthodox practice. As the number of families increased, they needed larger rooms.

In 1870, although still holding services in rented rooms on Main Street, the Jews of Harrisonburg formed a congregation and purchased a Torah for $100; a few years later the group received a charter in the name of the

Holsinger Studio Collection (#9862), Special Collections, Manuscript Division, University of Virginia Library

Bernard Oberdorfer left Germany in 1849 and arrived in Charlottesville as a peddler. After the Civil War, he was instrumental in establishing Charlottesville's Jewish congregation. Oberdorfer's Dry Goods on Main Street is shown here in 1916.

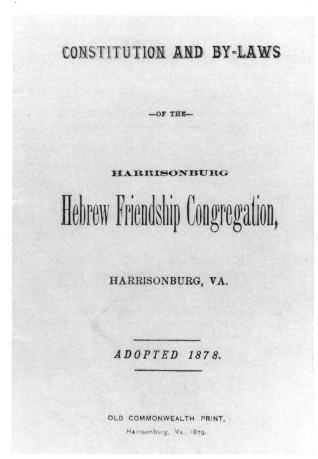

CONSTITUTION AND BY-LAWS

—OF THE—

HARRISONBURG

Hebrew Friendship Congregation,

HARRISONBURG, VA.

ADOPTED 1878.

OLD COMMONWEALTH PRINT,
Harrisonburg, Va., 1879.

Congregation Beth El, Harrisonburg

After several years of meeting in rented rooms, in 1870 the eleven Jewish families of Harrisonburg formed a congregation and received a charter in the name of the Hebrew Friendship Congregation. In 1891 the congregation, called Beth El, built a synagogue on North Main Street.

Hebrew Friendship Congregation. The bylaws, adopted a year later, noted that the business meetings "shall be conducted in English. If a member wishes to express his views in German, he shall have the privilege to do so." That year, the congregation counted eleven Jewish families and forty children. By 1890, the membership had climbed to ninety-three, and the following year the congregation built a synagogue on North Main Street, about two blocks from Court Square. In 1891 the congregation, called Beth El (House of God), began to worship in its new sanctuary and remained in that building until the 1960s. Over the ark holding the Torah scrolls were the tablets of the Ten Commandments, fashioned by Samuel Loewner.

When the first Jews settled in Staunton is not clear, and the early records do not indicate very much about them. It appears that individual merchants and peddlers lived in or came to the town before the Civil War and that enough Jews lived there to form a club in the late 1860s or early 1870s to help orient newcomers and provide charity for the needy. Congregation House of Israel organized in 1876 under the leadership of Major Alexander Hart and in 1884 bought the Hoover School on Kalorama Street for $600 to

Major Alexander Hart (1839–1911) of the 5th Louisiana settled in Virginia after the Civil War. Under his leadership, Congregation House of Israel was organized in Staunton in 1876. Because the small congregation could not afford to hire a rabbi, Hart, the first *parnas*, conducted the services for many years.

American Jewish Archives, Cincinnati

serve as a synagogue for Staunton and Waynesboro. The members of the congregation financed the purchase through a variety of fund-raising activities, including several raffles. After purchasing the building, the members did not have enough money to buy pews, so they used borrowed chairs for a while. The following year the congregation bought land for a cemetery. Although possessed of a sanctuary, the small congregation could not afford to hire a rabbi, and so Hart, the first president of House of Israel, conducted services for a number of years. There were lay leaders in Staunton until the 1930s.

Jewish growth in Fredericksburg proved very slow. Although early records indicate that individual Jews lived in the town as early as the 1770s, no viable community developed until well after the Civil War. Jewish settlers may have found greater economic opportunity in Richmond and also may have seen the established community there as a more congenial setting in which they could follow the precepts of their faith.

Some members of the Iseman family of Richmond moved to Fredericksburg just before the war and seem to have been responsible for other German Jews settling there. Records show that Fredericksburg Jews served in the Confederate army and that Isaac Hirsch, his father Kaufman, and his brother-in-law Benjamin Goldsmith ran a supplies company during the war. By 1870, they had each established individual companies in Fredericksburg: Kaufman Hirsch ran a grocery store, Isaac Hirsch a dry goods emporium, and Benjamin Goldsmith a clothing store. By the 1880s, more Jews had moved in. The older families established a Hebrew Aid Society to help the newcomers, and city directories listed an increasing number of Jewish businesses by the turn of the century. Fredericksburg, however, did not have a synagogue until well into the twentieth century, long after not only the Germans but also the next wave of immigrants, those from eastern Europe, had settled there.

In the Tidewater, there had been a continuous Jewish presence since the end of the eighteenth century, but by 1840, only two families remained. There had apparently at one time been enough Jews to provide a *minyan*, the ritual quorum needed for services, because in that year several Torah scrolls were found in a closet in a large house on Cumberland Street in Norfolk; no records, however, exist of any formal congregation. The arrival of the German Jews starting in the 1840s revivified the community. The late Malcolm Stern, the longtime dean of American Jewish genealogists who served for a time as rabbi of Ohef Sholom in Norfolk, credited the revival to Jacob Umstadter, who settled in the city in 1844. Umstadter had training both as a *schochet* (ritual butcher) and as a cantor, and his strong Orthodox background affected the local community.

Umstadter did not come alone. Within a few years the community had enough members to establish a congregation. On 22 October 1848, an organizing committee approved the renting of two rooms in the house of Nathan American for the purpose of holding religious services. A newcomer from Baltimore, Aaron Goldsmith, agreed to return to that city to secure a Torah scroll, and the members of the new and as yet unnamed congregation defrayed the cost by equal contributions among themselves.

The following year they elected Goldsmith as president and adopted the name Chevra B'nai Jaacov, which literally translated means "Association of the Sons of Jacob," but which they anglicized to "House of Jacob." Under the guidance of Goldsmith and of Jacob Umstadter, who served as *chazan*, or cantor, and led the religious services, the congregation grew swiftly, as more Jews settled in the city. In 1850 the congregation purchased land for a cemetery (still in use today), and in 1853, having outgrown the original two rooms, the House of Jacob rented the first floor of the Odd Fellows Hall on Wolf (now Market) Street near Avon. That same year, the General Assembly passed an act incorporating the trustees of the Hebrew and English Literary Institute in Norfolk, with a charter to provide instruction in both languages.

The growing congregation had been talking about erecting a synagogue in a building of its own, and that sentiment gained urgent impetus when the Odd Fellows Hall burned in February 1859. The following month the board purchased a lot on the east side of Cumberland and, with the help of a $1,760 mortgage, commissioned a brick building to serve as a permanent home. The members held their first services in the new synagogue before the end of the year.

The community survived the rigors of the Civil War fairly well only to succumb to the factionalization generated by the new spirit of Reform. In 1866 two men applied for the pulpit of the House of Jacob, one backed by the Reform group and the other by the traditionalist Orthodox faction. Neither got the job, and the following year peace seems to have been restored. The Reconstruction government required that all incorporated bodies secure a new charter, and the literary institute merged with the House of Jacob to form Congregation Ohef Sholom (Love of Peace).

Unfortunately, the members failed to live up to the name, and discord broke out as the Reformers gained an upper hand and began to initiate such changes as men and women sitting together. In February 1870, the more traditional members of Ohef Sholom resigned to form a new congregation, Beth-El, with the indomitable Jacob Umstadter as one of the founders. With the Orthodox faction gone, Ohef Sholom became a fully Reform congregation by adopting a new *minhag* (ritual), installing an organ, and having men and women sit together during services. By this time, Norfolk Jewry had grown large enough to support not only both the Reform Ohef Sholom and the Orthodox Beth-El, but also a nearby smaller community in Portsmouth.

One might have thought that Jews would have settled in northern Virginia earlier than the 1850s, given the location of the nation's capital, as

Collection of Norman Flayderman

After steady growth throughout the 1850s, the Jewish community in Alexandria founded a young men's literary association, a benevolent society, and a congregation. Officers announced the formation of Beth El in a letter to Isaac Leeser, editor and publisher of the monthly journal *Occident and American Jewish Advocate*.

well as the large Jewish community in nearby Baltimore. Although there is some evidence of individual Jews doing business in the port of Alexandria in the late eighteenth century, sustained Jewish life there dates only from the early 1850s with the arrival of immigrants from Bavaria, Württemberg, and other German areas. Some of them undertook peddling to make a living and could hardly be considered permanent residents. Lewis Sternheimer, for example, came to America in 1854, stayed in Alexandria for six months, later went to Australia, and finally settled in Richmond.

The number of Jews who actually settled in Alexandria is difficult to determine, because non-Jews often could not spell the strange German names. Leopold Genzberger, Lipmen Genzberg, Lipman Genzberger, Leibman Gainsburgh, Leyman Gentzburgh, Liebman Genzberger, Lippman Gunzberger, L. Gunzberg, and Luben Gentzberger might refer to no more than three people, and their separate identities can be established only because their wives had different names and their respective children can be identified.

The Jews who did settle in Alexandria opened dry goods stores on or near King Street and from the available evidence did not own slaves. What menial work had to be done in their businesses they either did themselves or hired other people to perform. Household help often consisted of single young German girls.

The Jewish population in Alexandria, like other parts of Virginia, grew steadily during the 1850s, and the community founded a young men's literary association, a charitable society, and then a synagogue. The Hebrew Benevolent Society, as in many other places, began as a dues-paying membership organization with two major responsibilities, helping its members when they faced times of need, such as during illness, and providing free, properly conducted Jewish burials for members and their immediate family in its own consecrated cemetery. To fulfill the latter obligation, the society bought a small plot from the Union Methodist Cemetery and dedicated it as the Home of Peace Cemetery. It has been enlarged several times and is still in use today. At some point, the society started making contributions to various charitable causes and also provided generous support to Beth El. (Today the society still exists, but no dues are collected; membership is based solely on ownership, by purchase or inheritance, of plots in Home of Peace Cemetery.)

Burying the dead proved far less contentious than praying with the living, as the establishment of the synagogue proved. Congregation Beth El dates to 1859, but it took two years of controversy to get it established. By the late 1850s, the Jews in Alexandria may have been divided fairly evenly between those who favored the traditional Orthodox ritual and those who supported the new Reform program. About this time the local newspaper ran a story that could have been written about the tensions then existing in Richmond and Norfolk as well as Alexandria. "There is some little difference," the reporter wrote,

Henry Hyman, a Richmond silversmith, watchmaker, jeweler, and importer, made this kiddush cup for his godson, Henry Levy, in 1851.

Beth Ahabah Museum and Archives

in conducting the religious services between the modern Jews, one part of them using the Hebrew and the other German, or whatever their native language may be. The last are we believe called reformers or progressives. To a reflecting Gentile, the sight of a religious assembly of these people is very interesting. Here we have the remnant of a once renowned nation firmly adhering to the custom of their fathers, which they have preserved amidst the greatest afflictions and calamities which ever befel a people.

In 1858 the Reformers sparked the controversy when they held services to celebrate Rosh Hashanah, the Jewish New Year, and limited the observance to one day instead of the Orthodox two-day commemoration.

The holiday was, in fact, celebrated only one day in ancient Israel, but after Jews were driven into exile by the Romans, they still tied their holidays to the Palestinian calendar. Living far from that land, they often could not tell exactly on which day certain holidays should be observed. To be sure they prayed at the right time, they adopted the practice of making these holidays into two-day affairs. The Reformers wanted to restore these holidays to one-day commemorations, and in modern Israel, where it is possible to know the calendar precisely, most holidays are also celebrated for one day.

The Orthodox protested against these practices, and one of them, adopting the older traditions of Thomas Jefferson and James Madison, wrote a letter to the local paper, the *Alexandria Gazette*. Using the pseudonym "Moses," he blasted the Reformers for their abandonment of traditional Judaism, especially the mixing of German with Hebrew, the latter being a holy language in which God had spoken to the original Moses. The Reformers won the day, and Beth El adopted the Reform *minhag*. Traditional Jews continued to go into Washington to pray at the Orthodox Washington Hebrew Congregation. There was not a traditional synagogue in Alexandria for more than fifty years, until the great wave of immigration came from eastern Europe.

The immigration from central Europe began in the late 1820s, accelerated in the 1830s, and was a veritable flood between 1840 and 1880. The Germans transformed the structure of Jewish communities not only in the northern cities but in Virginia as well. By the 1890s, the newcomers had firmly established themselves as communities in Norfolk, Charlottesville, Roanoke, Petersburg, and elsewhere and had overwhelmed the older established Beth Shalome of Richmond. Even in some smaller places, such as Lynchburg, Jewish communities existed, although being smaller than Richmond or Norfolk, it often took longer for them to organize a congregation. German Jews, for example, migrated into the Lynchburg area sometime after the Civil War but did not found a congregation until near the end of the century.

On 28 November 1897, twenty-three men gathered above Rosenthal's furniture store to create a congregation "to educate and train the children of the members thereof, and of such others as it may elect; and to aid and assist indigent and afflicted persons; to have a place of social meeting; and to engage in literary and benevolent pursuits." The organizers also agreed to raise funds to purchase a Torah scroll and to establish a quorum for regular Sabbath services. A committee set out to find a hall it could rent on a more permanent basis until the congregation could build a sanctuary of its own.

Within a few weeks a place had been found for Agudath Achim, the "Fellowship of Brothers," to meet, but unfortunately the fellowship soon split in two. Eleven of the twenty-three founders withdrew, took with them the Torah scroll, and established a new congregation, Ahavath Sholom (Love of Peace). But the rift made little sense. Lynchburg could hardly support two congregations, and the close business and personal ties among the town's Jews made them realize the foolishness of the split. In February 1899, the two congregations came together again and adopted the name Agudath Sholom, the "Fellowship of Peace."

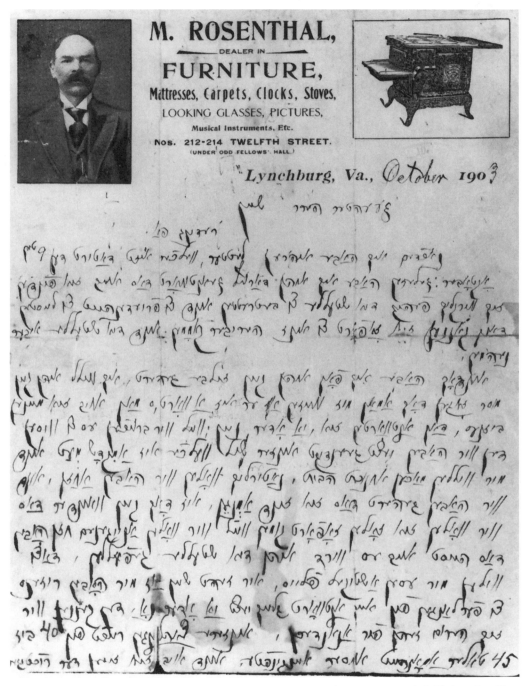

Congregation Agudath Sholom, Lynchburg

Congregation Agudath Sholom in Lynchburg, founded in 1897, had no regular rabbi until 1903, when M. Rosenthal, the first secretary of the congregation, wrote this letter to engage S. B. Schein of Reading, Pennsylvania, to fill the post. Schein served in Lynchburg for two years.

From that time on, Agudath Sholom followed the path of most of the other congregations in the smaller towns of Virginia. It had no regular rabbi for several years, until S. B. Schein of Reading, Pennsylvania, joined them in 1903. But Schein, although well liked by the congregation, stayed only two years; he left to study law and eventually had a distinguished career as a lawyer and judge in Wisconsin. After he left, the congregation had several rabbis. Then in 1917 David M. Somers came to town and for many years fulfilled several roles, including those of part-time rabbi, teacher, and *schochet*.

American Jewish Historical Society, Waltham, Massachusetts

Dr. Henry Hochheimer of Baltimore traveled in Virginia to Harrisonburg, Lynchburg, Danville, and other places to perform weddings between 1850 and 1900.

As with most new congregations, the great desire was to have a permanent synagogue. After meeting for six years in rented rooms, the congregation in July 1903 purchased the building of the First Christian Church on Church Street near Fifth. In some ways, this action marked a homecoming of sorts, because in the 1870s the First Christian Church had rented some rooms for devotional purposes to a small group of Jews who had settled in Lynchburg after the Civil War.

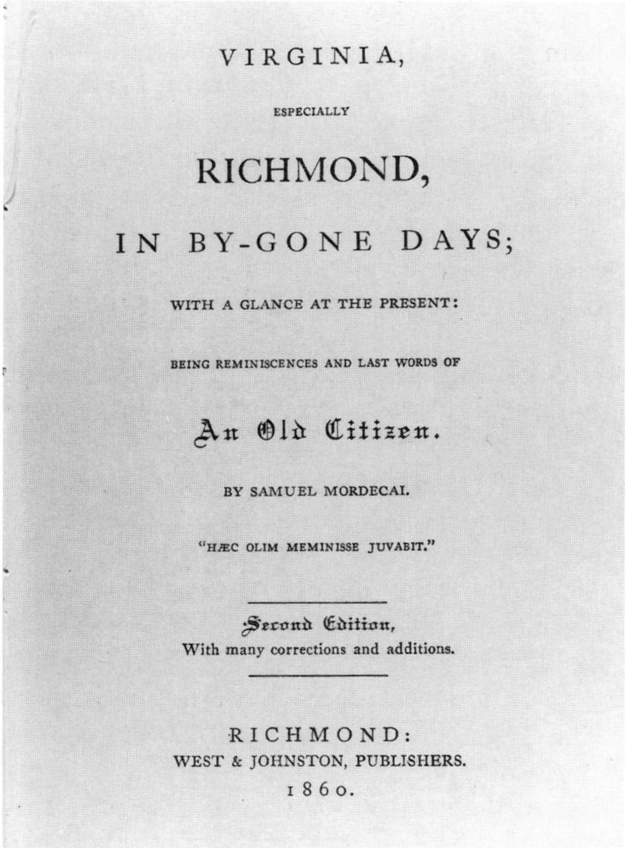

VIRGINIA,

ESPECIALLY

RICHMOND,

IN BY-GONE DAYS;

WITH A GLANCE AT THE PRESENT:

BEING REMINISCENCES AND LAST WORDS OF

An Old Citizen.

BY SAMUEL MORDECAI.

"HÆC OLIM MEMINISSE JUVABIT."

Second Edition,
With many corrections and additions.

RICHMOND:
WEST & JOHNSTON, PUBLISHERS.
1860.

Samuel Mordecai (1786–1865), a merchant in Petersburg and Richmond, published a second edition of his classic chronicle of Richmond's history in 1860.

Virginia Historical Society

Although Virginia did not attract as many of the immigrants as did northern cities, those who did come to the Old Dominion found a hospitable environment. The state that had enacted Thomas Jefferson's Statute for Religious Freedom saw the Jews as one more of many religious groups and saw individual Jews as productive citizens who enriched the community and the commonwealth. In many places, small congregations could not have built their synagogues without help from their Christian neighbors, help generously given.

In fact, Christian help proved remarkably strong on one issue at this time. During the 1840s there arose a movement to declare America formally "a Christian nation." As part of this movement, certain groups pushed either to enact Sunday closing laws or to enforce those that had been on the books, some of them since colonial days. Although one could expect Jews to protest such laws, a number of Christians did so as well. Congressman Richard M. Johnson of Kentucky (later Martin Van Buren's vice-president) told the House of Representatives in 1830 that "the

Constitution regards the conscience of the Jew as sacred as that of the Christian." In Virginia a Protestant minister, William S. Plumer, published a pamphlet entitled *The Substance of an Argument Against the Indiscriminate Incorporation of Churches and Religious Societies* (1846) in which he responded to petitions to the General Assembly to provide aid to Christian sects. In tones clearly reminiscent of Jeffersonian ideals, he charged that even if such aid could be distributed fairly to the more than twenty Christian denominations having churches in Virginia, such assistance would be unfair to Jews, atheists, and "the great mass of men indifferent to all forms of religion."

In 1845 the Jews of Richmond petitioned for the repeal of a city ordinance that added additional penalties to a state law dealing with violation of the Christian Sabbath. The law had been drafted primarily to restrict the movement of slaves and free blacks but penalized those who kept their shops open. The Jews phrased their protest in broad terms of religious freedom. The ordinance, they maintained, violated their constitutional rights as Virginians, especially the principle of equal treatment under the law. Such laws were "but the beginning of a revolution backwards, to abridge the rights of individuals, which have been opened as wide as the gates of mercy, by the sages of the Revolution." Whether because of the logic of the argument or because of the influence of Jewish merchants, the city fathers soon repealed the ordinance.

That some anti-Semitism existed cannot be denied, and the war that broke upon the nation in the spring of 1861 exacerbated that prejudice. Yet the Jews who had come to Virginia, like others before them, saw the Old Dominion as their home. As did their neighbors, they marched off to fight, and especially in the Valley, like their neighbors, sometimes brothers fought on opposing sides. The war and Reconstruction that followed wreaked havoc on all Virginians, and it is one sign of the strength of the newly established Jewish communities that they survived the turmoil and grew stronger during the ordeal.

SLAVES AND WAR

THE Civil War caused great hardship and devastation in the Old Dominion, and the Jews of Virginia shared the pain and anguish of their Christian neighbors. Jew and gentile alike flocked to the colors. They served and died in the Lost Cause. The destruction of the economy caused many Jewish merchants to lose their stores, their merchandise, and their fortunes. As they surveyed the ashes of Richmond in the spring of 1865, or the ruin of once proud plantations along the James, or the vandalism of raiders in the Valley, they had little choice but to pick up whatever they could find and begin anew.

The most unusual part of the story of Jews in Virginia during the Civil War is just how common their experience was. There is little to differentiate Jewish history from the larger context of Virginia history in the years leading up to the war and continuing through Reconstruction. Jews, like their gentile neighbors, had owned and traded in slaves; they initially differed over secession, but once the decision had been made, they supported it with blood and money; they gave aid to the Army of Northern Virginia and appeared to have enlisted in as great if not a greater proportion of their numbers as the general population; the women served as nurses and sheltered the wounded in their homes; and after the war they had to rebuild their lives as well. The stories that are told of Jews are the same as those told about Christians. In only one area does the tale differ, and that involves the first overt manifestations of anti-Semitism in the Old Dominion.

In colonial days Jews throughout the colonies owned slaves, as did most of their middle-class neighbors. A tax register of Richmond citizens for 1788 shows ten Jews on the roll of 360, and all but one of them had a domestic slave, and one household had three. In the seventeenth and eighteenth centuries, most Americans accepted slavery as a normal condition. Moreover, many whites, including Jews, had initially come to America as indentured servants, a condition that although limited in duration was little better than bondage.

Only a small number of Jews in the Old South owned plantations and derived their living from the land. In fact, Judah P. Benjamin, the owner of

Courtesy of Richard Bendheim

In July 1858, Joseph Myers of Richmond insured his slave Jordan with American Life Insurance and Trust Company. For a premium of $13.12, Myers received $800 coverage.

Belle Chasse, a great house outside New Orleans, was an exception to this rule, and he made his money not from agriculture but from the law. Within Virginia, some families possessed plantations, but most of the Jews in the state lived in towns and kept stores. Although census records are incomplete, analysis of them indicates that in the 1840s and 1850s about one in four Jews owned slaves, about the same proportion as that of the southern white populace.

At Passover, when Jews retell the story of the Exodus, they are reminded that they were once "slaves to Pharaoh in Egypt" and therefore have a moral obligation to treat others as they would wish to be treated themselves. Although the ancient Hebrews themselves owned slaves, religious obligations greatly limited this practice, and scholars believe that the actual institution had all but disappeared by the destruction of the First Temple in the sixth century B.C.E.

How Jewish slave owners treated their bondsmen and women is hard to discern, and probably the only generalization that is safe to make is that some owners treated their slaves well and some did not. We can find evidence for both situations. When Mary Gerst wrote to her husband during the war, she often noted that "all the Negroes desire to be remembered to you." Emma Mordecai, who moved to North Carolina after the war, received a letter in 1867 from one of her former slaves, Sarah Norris, who sent news of family and friends in Richmond. Moreover, she assured the Mordecais that she and her husband were tending the family graves in the Richmond Jewish cemetery. "I could never forget my people," she wrote. "I loved them then, I love them now." And although there is also evidence of manumission by Jews, there are instances in which owners broke up families to sell off slaves at a profit. Again, the story is little different from that in Virginia as a whole, or even in the South.

There can be no denying that Jews engaged in the buying and selling of blacks, whom they and the white population at large considered a commodity. One writer, in fact, charged that Jews advocated the secession of southern states from the Union in order to protect their interest in the slave trade and cited as proof of this motivation the assertion that Jews owned the largest slave auction house in Richmond. There were, in fact, five Jews listed as slave traders in Richmond in 1860—Benjamin Davis, Solomon Davis, J. B. Davis, Ash Levy, and Samuel Reese—but another source indicates that only three out of the seventy-four slave traders in Richmond on the eve of the war were Jewish. The largest, the Davis clan of Richmond and Petersburg, had started out as peddlers and then specialized in slaves, but, according to historian Jacob Rader Marcus, "the sales of all Jewish traders lumped together did not equal that of the one Gentile firm dominant in the business." Given the large percentage of Jews who went into retailing, the proportion specializing in slaves is actually quite low.

Some of this low incidence may be attributed to moral aversion, but one has to keep in mind the fact that although immigrants starting out in business could raise enough capital to stock a wagon or a small store with dry goods, the buying and selling of slaves required cash resources far beyond the reach of most newcomers.

Why did a people who annually recalled their own slavery not take a more pronounced opposition to the peculiar institution? Except in regard to religion, where Jews fought for their freedom, they tended to accept the United States and to enjoy the freedom it offered to them—a freedom unique in the entire world and in their long history. Jews wanted more than anything else to be accepted in return, to be "a part and not apart." They dressed, acted, and lived like their neighbors, and if they resided in the South, they tended to take on the mores and attitudes of the region. Even if Jews had decided to oppose slavery, it would have been a very risky proposition. In Virginia, for example, the Jewish population barely exceeded two thousand souls on the eve of the war, perhaps one-tenth of 1 percent of the population. Discretion seemed the key to survival.

In one area, however, Jews did differ a bit from their neighbors. Many small Jewish shopkeepers catered to blacks, a practice most Christian store owners avoided, because many whites believed that letting blacks into a store amounted to little more than an invitation to shoplifting. Both before and after the war, and even during the era of Jim Crow, Jewish stores were often the only ones willing to serve black customers.

The problem of slavery became increasingly sectional and bitter in the 1850s. The North in general wanted to limit the practice to where it already existed in the southern states and prevent its spread into the western territories. The abolitionist argument against slavery anywhere enjoyed support among only a relatively small part of the population. The South, on the other hand, not only defended its peculiar institution but also wanted assurances that as the nation grew slavery would be protected everywhere. By the time of the 1860 election, Abraham Lincoln could accurately describe the United States as "a house divided."

A few rabbis in the North, most notably Bernhard Felsenthal of Chicago, actively took the abolitionist position. A majority, like most northerners, cared little about slavery in the South but wanted to block its expansion. In the South there were few rabbis at that time because there were still few congregations that could afford full-time clerical leaders. But Maximilian Michelbacher of Richmond's Beth Ahabah, like his Christian colleagues, saw slavery as divinely ordained. In an 1863 sermon praying for God to aid the Confederacy, Michelbacher said of slavery, "The man servants and maid servants Thou has given unto us, that we may be merciful to them in righteousness and bear rule over them, the enemy are attempting to seduce, that they, too, may turn against us, whom Thou has appointed over them as instructors in Thy wise dispensation."

Virginia Jews also differed little from their neighbors regarding the desirability of secession in the winter of 1860–61, but once the decision had been reached, Virginians rallied to the cause of their state. When the state convention voted to leave the Union in April 1861, its leaders called on William Flegenheimer to inscribe the ordinance of secession. During the war the Confederate government used Flegenheimer's calligraphic skills to draw up the credentials of its overseas ministers, and he himself worked for a while as an assistant to the treasurer of the post office.

Men flocked to the Stars and Bars, and the two leading Richmond militia groups, the Blues and the Grays, both had significant Jewish membership. In Petersburg, Norfolk, and elsewhere the story was the same: whether they owned slaves or not, nearly all Virginia Jews supported the state's decision to secede, and the men joined the army to defend that decision. Myer Angle, the first president of Beth Ahabah, saw all six of his sons go off to fight for the Confederacy. There is no need to list all the Jews who fought for the South; that job has been done elsewhere. Suffice it to say that enough gave their lives that Richmond set apart a special Soldiers' Section in the Hebrew Cemetery containing thirty-one graves of both Richmond and non-Richmond men, which until after World War II was the only Jewish military cemetery in the world. The railing around the enclosure represents the arms of the branches of the Confederate service: muskets for infantry, sabers for cavalry, and artillery kepis.

Some of the stories of individuals, however, are worth retelling. Just before the war Henry Gintzberger arrived in Salem. An itinerant peddler in his mid-twenties, he may have been the first Jew ever seen in that small Virginia town, and his arrival seems to have become a legend in town lore. Soon after his appearance in Salem, he fell sick with a high fever. The local townspeople would not allow a stranger to go unattended, and one of the residents took Gintzberger into his house, where the family nursed him through a long illness. By the time he had recovered, the war had broken out. Perhaps to show his gratitude to the people of Salem, Gintzberger enlisted with the other men of the town in the Salem Flying Artillery, and he served with the unit until killed in action at Cold Harbor in 1864.

The great sculptor Sir Moses Ezekiel remembered vividly all his life his experiences as a cadet at the Virginia Military Institute, when he and his unit participated in the battle of New Market. Later he went with his fellow cadets to Capitol Square in Richmond, where after a parade and a speech by the governor praising their heroism, the state presented the corps with a new flag. "Ten of our boys were killed in the battle of Newmarket," he

Rosa, thou dearest of my heart,

Only to thee my love can I impart,

Sacred and holy is my vow,

And humbly now before thy shrine I bow.

Can my love for thee be in vain?

Oh! dearest spare my heart from such a pain;

Hope bids me from all doubts refrain,

Nor cease my efforts thy pure love to gain._

Richmond Va.
July 6.th 60.

W. Flegenheimer.

William Flegenheimer, who later engrossed Virginia's ordinance of secession, composed and decorated this message in July 1860 for the woman he married in the fateful month of April 1861. The first letter in each line spells the name of his fiancée.

recalled. "It was later one of the most sacred duties in my life to remodel my bronze statue of *Virginia Mourning Her Dead* to be placed on the parade ground of the V.M.I., overlooking the graves of my dead comrades, so that

The Confederate section of the Hebrew Cemetery in Richmond, enclosed by a wrought iron fence representing the branches of the armed forces, contains thirty-one graves. Until well after World War II, it was the only Jewish military cemetery in the world.

their memory may go on in imperishable bronze, sounding their heroism and Virginia's memory down through all ages and forever."

If Ezekiel remembered the gallantry and pageantry, others recalled great anguish. Isaac Hirsch of Fredericksburg joined Company A of Virginia's 30th Infantry Regiment in May 1861, and he kept a diary of his experiences during the war. He saw some action at minor skirmishes at Aquia and Manassas, but after a particularly bloody fight near Warrenton, he wrote, "I left the field (of blackened bodies) with a heavy heart, as I had never seen the Romance of War in this shape before. . . . I got back to camp a wiser man than I had left it." After he mustered out in the fall of 1863, his last entry read, "Got home last night. Thank God. Home once more."

Major Edmund Trowbridge Dane Myers (a founder of the RF&P Railroad) wrote his uncle, Sam Mordecai, about his apprehensions concerning the wisdom of secession, but, he noted, "I am with [Virginia]—bound to her for the issue be it for weal or for woe." Sam's brother, Captain Alfred Mordecai, also agonized over what to do. Nearly all of his close relatives lived in Virginia or North Carolina, and they wrote to him begging that he give up his position as head of the Watervliet Arsenal in upstate New York

Richmond-born Moses Ezekiel (1844–1917), a veteran of the battle of New Market, sculpted *Virginia Mourning Her Dead* for the Virginia Military Institute and a memorial for the Confederate dead at Arlington National Cemetery. Although he was rewarded abroad with knighthoods from Wilhelm I of Germany and Victor Emmanuel II and Humbert I of Italy, he complained that "my own city & state have added more towards the endeavour to crush me than any other place."

Beth Ahabah Museum and Archives

and return home to serve the Confederacy. Mordecai received and refused offers of a commission in the Rebel army, one from Jefferson Davis himself. He no doubt found it difficult to turn down the entreaties of his sister Ellen, who lived in Richmond. She implored, "I feel with every member of our family and all our friends that you should come where you are not only desired but needed in directing the military affairs of your native state."

Despite his attachments to the South, Captain Mordecai felt a sense of loyalty to the Union he had served and also to the sensibilities of his northern-born wife, Sara. He had no sympathy for the abolition movement, but he would not oppose the country that had treated him so well; at the same time, he could not fight against his brethren. In the end, he resigned his commission but refused to take up arms for either North or South, a decision that reflected his moral standards but that angered both sides in the conflict.

Other families in Richmond and indeed throughout Virginia and the South faced similar internal tension. Jacob A. Levy had two sons who fought for their state, Captain E. J. Levy of the Richmond Blues and Private Isaac J. Levy, who fell in battle near Petersburg in 1864. Two of Levy's

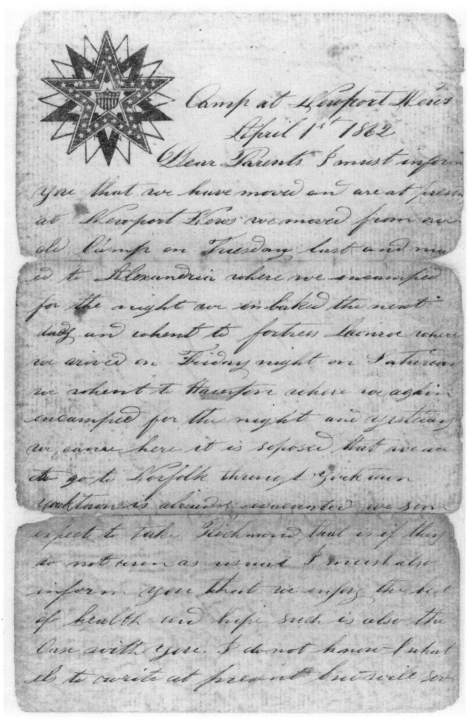

Joseph Kline wrote to his parents from the camp of Company I of the 17th Virginia Infantry in Newport News on the eve of the Peninsula campaign.

nephews, however, Abraham I. Levy and Jacob E. Hyneman, chose to serve in the Union army. Jacob Ezekiel, despite his son's passion for the war, remained a staunch Unionist, but because both his sons had enlisted in the Confederate army, he could not leave Richmond. He remained in business, doing what he could to help Yankees captured and incarcerated in Libby Prison. In Charlottesville, Isaac Leterman fought for the Union and his younger brother Simon for the rebellion, while Simon's wife, Hannah, served as a Confederate nurse.

In general, Jews, like other southerners, rushed to enlist. Adjutant General Samuel Cooper estimated that Jews made up a significant portion of some units, and on two occasions Robert E. Lee had to refuse High Holiday furloughs for Jewish troops on the grounds that their absence would greatly weaken his forces. On at least one of those occasions, the request came from Maximilian Michelbacher, who also pleaded with Lee to commute the sentence of a young Jewish soldier, Private Isaac Arnold of the 8th Alabama Regiment, whom a court-martial had found guilty of cowardice under fire and sentenced to death. Michelbacher did not question the integrity of the court but asked that justice be tempered with mercy. On this occasion, he apparently succeeded, at least in regard to the unfortunate Arnold, but Michelbacher could not get Lee to allow Jewish troops furlough for Passover. As the general noted, "I think it more than probable that the army will be engaged in active operations, when, of course, no one would wish to be absent from its ranks."

Lee apparently tried to help on such requests whenever he could. When a Richmond soldier asked leave to attend services at the synagogue, his captain refused and marked on the letter: "Disapproved. If such applications were granted, the whole army would turn Jews or shaking Quakers." But when the papers came to Lee's desk, he granted the request and returned it to the captain "with the advice that he should always respect the religious views and feelings of others."

Michelbacher, according to several sources, served in all but name as a chaplain for Jewish soldiers in the Confederate army, although he never wore the uniform. He constantly visited the various army units camped near Richmond, seeking out Jewish soldiers but speaking to all who needed comfort. Michelbacher could have been a chaplain had he wanted to, because the Confederate Congress, in the act establishing military chaplains, merely required that they be "clergymen," with no denominational limitations. As Bertram Korn noted, "there was probably not a sufficient number of Jews in any one Confederate regiment to warrant the appointment of a Jewish chaplain, but at least there was no *legal* barrier to such an

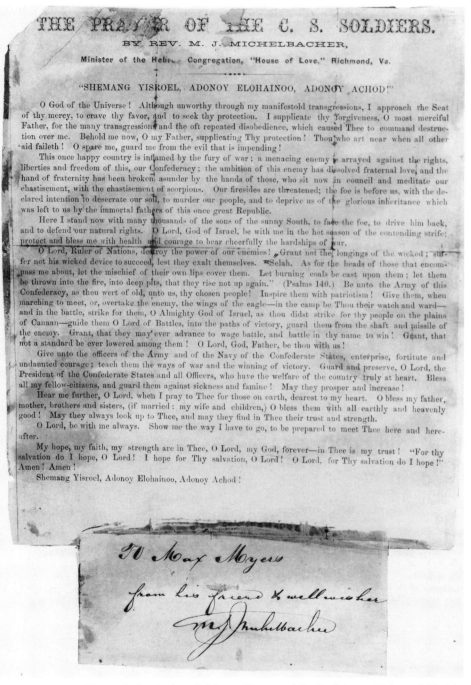

THE PRAYER OF THE C. S. SOLDIERS.

BY REV. M. J. MICHELBACHER,

Minister of the Hebr__ Congregation, "House of Love," Richmond, Va.

"SHEMANG YISROEL, ADONOY ELOHAINOO, ADONOY ACHOD!"

O God of the Universe! Although unworthy through my manifestold transgressions, I approach the Seat of thy mercy, to crave thy favor, and to seek thy protection. I supplicate thy forgiveness, O most merciful Father, for the many transgressions and the oft repeated disobedience, which caused Thee to command destruction over me. Behold me now, O my Father, supplicating Thy protection! Thou who art near when all other aid faileth! O spare me, guard me from the evil that is impending!

This once happy country is inflamed by the fury of war; a menacing enemy is arrayed against the rights, liberties and freedom of this, our Confederacy; the ambition of this enemy has dissolved fraternal love, and the hand of fraternity has been broken asunder by the hands of those, who sit now in council and meditate our chastisement, with the chastisement of scorpions. Our firesides are threatened; the foe is before us, with the declared intention to desecrate our soil, to murder our people, and to deprive us of the glorious inheritance which was left to us by the immortal fathers of this once great Republic.

Here I stand now with many thousands of the sons of the sunny South, to face the foe, to drive him back, and to defend our natural rights. O Lord, God of Israel, be with me in the hot season of the contending strife; protect and bless me with health and courage to bear cheerfully the hardships of war.

O Lord, Ruler of Nations, destroy the power of our enemies! Grant not the longings of the wicked; suffer not his wicked device to succeed, lest they exalt themselves. Selah. As for the heads of those that encompass me about, let the mischief of their own lips cover them. Let burning coals be cast upon them; let them be thrown into the fire, into deep pits, that they rise not up again." (Psalms 140.) Be unto the Army of this Confederacy, as thou wert of old, unto us, thy chosen people! Inspire them with patriotism! Give them, when marching to meet, or, overtake the enemy, the wings of the eagle—in the camp be Thou their watch and ward—and in the battle, strike for them, O Almighty God of Israel, as thou didst strike for thy people on the plains of Canaan—guide them O Lord of Battles, into the paths of victory, guard them from the shaft and missile of the enemy. Grant, that they may ever advance to wage battle, and battle in thy name to win! Grant, that not a standard be ever lowered among them! O Lord, God, Father, be thou with us!

Give unto the officers of the Army and of the Navy of the Confederate States, enterprise, fortitude and undaunted courage; teach them the ways of war and the winning of victory. Guard and preserve, O Lord, the President of the Confederate States and all Officers, who have the welfare of the country truly at heart. Bless all my fellow-citizens, and guard them against sickness and famine! May they prosper and increase!

Hear me further, O Lord, when I pray to Thee for those on earth, dearest to my heart. O bless my father, mother, brothers and sisters, (if married: my wife and children,) O bless them with all earthly and heavenly good! May they always look up to Thee, and may they find in Thee their trust and strength.

O Lord, be with me always. Show me the way I have to go, to be prepared to meet Thee here and hereafter.

My hope, my faith, my strength are in Thee, O Lord, my God, forever—in Thee is my trust! "For thy salvation do I hope, O Lord! I hope for Thy salvation, O Lord! O Lord, for Thy salvation do I hope!" Amen! Amen!

Shemang Yisroel, Adonoy Elohainoo, Adonoy Achod!

Eleanor S. Brockenbrough Library, Museum of the Confederacy, Richmond, Virginia; photograph by Katherine Wetzel

Maximilian J. Michelbacher inscribed a copy of his "Prayer of the C.S. Soldiers" for Max Myers. The prayer asks the "Almighty God of Israel" to guide the southern warriors "into the paths of victory, guard them from the shaft and missile of the enemy. Grant, that they may ever advance to wage battle, and battle in thy name to win!"

appointment." There is no evidence that any rabbi served formally as a chaplain, although Louis Ginsberg maintains that Uriah Feibelman of the Petersburg Grays was appointed chaplain in Mahone's Brigade of the Army of Northern Virginia and served for two years.

The need for charitable work during the war increased manyfold. In Richmond, Beth Shalome and Beth Ahabah agreed to work together to provide relief for the poor of the city, especially the Jewish poor. The burden of this work, however, fell on the women, whose role in the Civil War must not be overlooked. Although women have always suffered when their fathers, husbands, and sons have gone off to fight and to die, very often the field of battle has been far away. In the Civil War, fighting took place in Virginia throughout all four years of the conflict, with especially heavy fighting around Richmond. Women did the usual things, such as sewing items soldiers needed, but they also worked in hospitals, took care of the wounded in their homes, and often went without food so they could feed the famished soldiers stationed in the city. At Beth Shalome, women met in the basement of the Mayo Street building nearly every day to make clothes for the army, while the women of Beth Ahabah performed similar work nearby at Marshall and Eleventh.

Because so much of the fighting took place nearby, very often women knew that their husbands or sons were encamped in the vicinity and would go to see them, or at least try to do so. Years after the war, Rosena Hutzler Levy recalled going to the camps, getting permission from the officers, worrying when she learned her husband had been captured, and then, after he had been exchanged and quite ill, bringing him home to nurse. Mary Gerst, on the other hand, declined her husband's suggestion that she come to see him at his camp in Ashland, declaring that "I do not think a military camp is any place for ladies."

A relative newcomer to Richmond, the widowed Phoebe Yates Pember, once a South Carolina belle, went to work as an aide in the large Chimborazo Hospital and was soon made superintendent of one of the wings. Her zeal for the southern cause knew no bounds, and she defiantly wrote in *A Southern Woman's Story*: "At last I lifted my voice and congratulated myself at being born of a nation and religion that did not enjoin forgiveness of its enemies, that enjoyed the privilege of praying for an eye for an eye." Given the size of the Jewish community, she no doubt made the acquaintance of Emma Mordecai, who was an equally fierce devotee of the cause. Mordecai acquiesced to family pressure in the spring of 1864 and moved out of Richmond to Rosewood, an estate her brother and sister-in-law owned nearby, and there she began keeping a diary. It tells

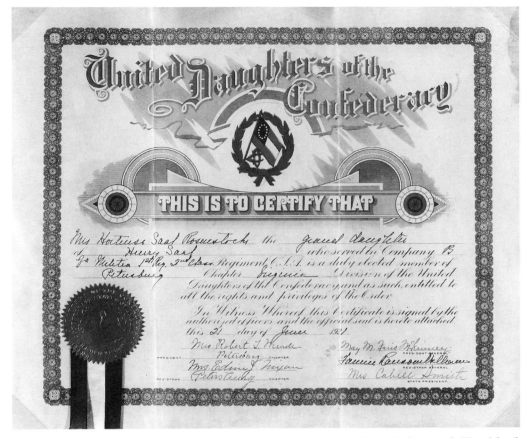

Louis A. Rosenstock III and family

In 1921 Hortense Saal Rosenstock was admitted to the Petersburg chapter of the United Daughters of the Confederacy through the military service of her grandfather, Henry Saal. Saal saw action in Company B of the 1st Virginia Militia.

about her many visits to the Camp Winder Hospital and how often soldiers stopped by the farm for food or just a drink of water. On 18 June 1864, she recorded:

> The usual thronging to the house all day, but this disturbed Rose [her sister-in-law] no more than it did me. She is so kind & indulgent to our soldiers that she thinks nothing a trouble that she can do for them, & never refuses them anything if she can possibly spare it. One of them left a poor broken-down horse here to be taken care of. He had some bad sores, which Rose & I had well washed and dressed, & she had him well grazed in the garden walks. He had 'U.S.' branded on him, but I have no hatred of the Yankee *horses*. . . . Heard heavy cannonading all day, & men who were on guard duty say they heard it all last night.

Rose and Emma Mordecai, of course, had to be in charge of the farm, a situation common throughout the South during the war. Mary Gerst took over the running of Glennmary and often wrote to her husband that work on the farm went on as usual, although the overabundance of rain made her worry about the crops.

One should not think that Jewish women ministered only to Jewish soldiers and that the Christian women of Richmond took care of only wounded Christians. The women—Jew and Christian—who went to the hospitals took care of all in need. It is true that Jewish homes particularly welcomed Jewish soldiers and offered them something that their neighbors could not—a place where they could observe Jewish ritual and feel at home. But the women took care of soldiers in need, and one story told by Herbert T. Ezekiel and Gaston Lichtenstein illustrates this concern well:

> Major Alexander Hart, of the Fifth Louisiana . . . was terribly wounded in one of his legs. So severe was the injury that the surgeon said recovery was impossible, and wanted to take off the limb forthwith. A splendid lady, to whose house he had been carried, begged the surgeon to spare the leg for a few days at least, and she would give the wound her personal attention. So young and handsome a man . . . should not lose a leg. True to her promise, she nursed him back to health, still the happy possessor of two good limbs. The Major always endeavored to visit his friend every year. On one occasion when he was stopping at her house a daughter-in-law complained that there was no ham on the table and started to get some. 'No,' said the old lady, 'there shall be no ham on my table when my "Jewish son" (as she always lovingly called him) is here.'

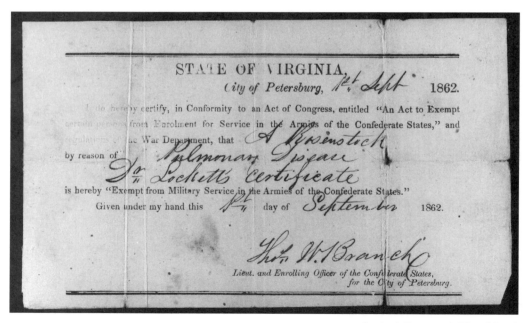

Louis A. Rosenstock III and family

Anthony Rosenstock, owner of a dry goods store in Petersburg, received a certificate exempting him from Confederate military service because of pulmonary disease.

No doubt as a result in part of this act of generosity, Hart stayed on in Richmond for a while after the war. He married Leonora Levy, the youngest daughter of Jacob A. Levy, the man whose two sons fought on the Confederate side and his two nephews for the Union.

One would like to believe, and there is evidence to do so, that this act of selfless kindness by a Christian woman to a young Jewish soldier is a far more accurate reflection of what most Virginians felt toward their Jewish neighbors than the mindless diatribes of a handful of bigots.

In both North and South the war triggered anti-Semitic sentiments that had been, for the most part, relatively absent before 1861. Although there had been a growth in nativist sentiment in the 1830s and 1840s that had expressed itself in the Know-Nothing party, for the most part that prejudice had been aimed at the Irish Catholics who came to America in large numbers starting in the 1820s. In Virginia the only overt example of anti-Semitism was the publication in 1828 of "Judith Bensaddi," a pernicious story by the Reverend Henry Ruffner. Ruffner, a well-known preacher in the Valley and president of Washington College (now Washington and Lee University), painted an unflattering portrait of Jews as, he maintained, Christians saw them. There were, at the time, only a handful of Jews in the Valley, and the diary of Alexander Hart and the experiences of the Loewner family in Harrisonburg seem to indicate they enjoyed good relations with their Christian neighbors.

Economic tensions, personal fears and frustrations, and the mass passions generated by war required an outlet, however, and in the past the victim of these conditions had often been Jews. The Civil War generated the same emotional needs. Although we can clearly document outbursts of hatred of Jews, we must also note that given the ferocity of the war, the manifestations were comparatively mild—there were no pogroms on either side—and, perhaps more important, not only did Jews openly oppose the prejudice, but non-Jews also came to their defense.

In the North, Congress initially required that chaplains in the Union army "be a regularly ordained minister of some Christian denomination," but Rabbi Arnold Fischel of New York, who had been disqualified as a chaplain of Cameron's Dragoons under this clause, approached Lincoln to protest. The president promised to help, and in July 1862 Congress changed the offensive phrase to read "some religious denomination."

Six months later came the single most blatant act of anti-Semitism that occurred in nineteenth-century America. On 17 December 1862, Ulysses S. Grant, commanding general of the Department of the Tennessee, issued General Order No. 11 expelling all Jews from that area within twenty-four hours. Grant asserted that the Jews violated every regulation of trade and therefore undermined the war effort. All Jews not leaving were to be arrested. In Holly Springs, Mississippi (Grant's headquarters), and in a few other towns, Order No. 11 was enforced. But in Paducah, Kentucky, Cesar Kaskel and others sent Lincoln a telegram, and then Kaskel went to Washington to plead his people's case. Lincoln saw Kaskel on 3 January 1863—two days after the Emancipation Proclamation went into effect—and immediately ordered General in Chief Henry W. Halleck to have Grant's order rescinded.

Charles Francis Adams, who served as Union minister to Great Britain during the conflict, noted in his diary a conversation he had had on the eve of the war with Senator Andrew Johnson of Tennessee, later president following Lincoln's death. Adams records Johnson as saying: "There's that [David] Yulee, miserable little cuss! I remember him in the House—the contemptible little Jew—standing there and begging us—yes! begging us to let Florida in as a state . . . and now that despicable little beggar stands up in the Senate and talks about *her* rights." After finishing with Yulee, Johnson started in on Judah P. Benjamin: "There's another Jew—that miserable Benjamin! He looks on a country and a government as he would on a suit of old clothes. He sold out the old one; and he would sell out the new if he could in so doing make two or three millions." The prominence of Yulee and Benjamin in Rebel ranks led some northerners to assert that all Jews were secessionists and that there would never have been a rebellion had Jewish bankers not planned it in order to enhance their profits.

There were also instances of anti-Semitism in the Confederacy. For example, Senator Henry S. Foote of Tennessee, a native of Fauquier County, Virginia, proposed to amend Tennessee's constitution to ban Jews from coming within twelve miles of the capital. Such expressions, however, were rare. The Confederate Congress did not exclude non-Christians when establishing chaplaincies, and no southern general attempted to exile Jews from areas under his command. In Virginia, invitations went to rabbis as well as to Christian ministers to offer prayers at the beginning of the legislative day, and when some groups tried to secure special privileges for Christians, the efforts always failed under a barrage of criticism invoking the names of Jefferson and Madison and references to the Statute for Religious Freedom. But anti-Semitism existed, some of it, ironically, sparked by the same Judah P. Benjamin who so angered Andrew Johnson.

Benjamin had been born on St. Thomas in the Virgin Islands of British parents who later moved to Charleston, South Carolina. He attended Yale and then became a successful lawyer in New Orleans. Although he never converted or denied his Jewish birth, Benjamin took no interest in Jewish affairs, and there is no record of his ever belonging to a synagogue; nonetheless, he was identified by both friend and foe as a

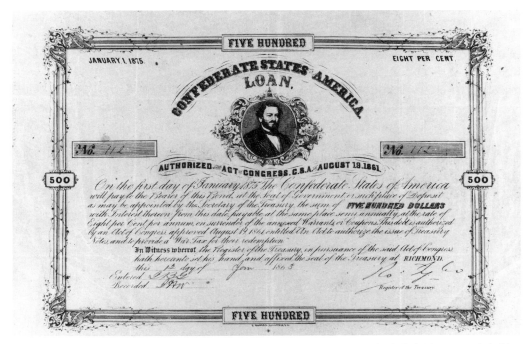

Beth Ahabah Museum and Archives

This Confederate bond, redeemable in January 1875 at 8 percent interest, features a portrait of Judah P. Benjamin (1811–1884), who served in the Confederate cabinet as attorney general, secretary of war, and secretary of state. While in Richmond, Benjamin took no part in the life of the Jewish community.

Jew. Elected to the United States Senate in 1852, Benjamin sided with the secessionists and served in the Confederate cabinet as attorney general, secretary of war, and secretary of state. After the war, he moved to England rather than live in the defeated South, and there he became a distinguished barrister.

Whereas northerners attacked Benjamin as a secessionist, southern anti-Semites tended to blame him for all the ills of the Confederacy. A letter to the editor of the *Richmond Enquirer* believed it blasphemous for a Jew to hold so high an office and maintained that southern prayers would be better received by the Almighty if Benjamin were ousted from the cabinet. President Jefferson Davis once found himself assailed in violent language by a Virginian because he had appointed a Jew to his cabinet. Davis steadfastly opposed this and all other attempts to get rid of Benjamin, whose abilities he recognized and valued and whom he counted as a friend.

Much as northerners charged Jews with profiteering, so too did southerners, often with Benjamin as their target. The Union blockade of southern ports led to severe shortages, and many people engaged in hoarding, smuggling, and profiteering. Although blockade running has often been made out to be a romance of high adventure, in fact it was a dangerous and far from glamorous venture. Philip Whitlock, a tailor in private life and quartermaster clerk with the Richmond Grays who had been present at the hanging of John Brown, recounted in his diary how he and his brother-in-law, Ellis Abram, decided to run the blockade along with four colleagues. They had no trouble getting to the Potomac, where they found a black man willing to row them over. Moving with muffled oars, they spotted a Union gunboat when they were halfway across. The oarsman wanted to turn back, but one of the passengers convinced him to continue by putting a revolver to his head. Whitlock and Abram made their way to New York, where they stayed for nearly a week buying notions that would fit into their hand luggage. They filled their bags with fine-toothed combs, tobacco pipes, pins, needles, pencils, and other small goods and then headed home.

This proved an even more arduous journey than they had expected, and the two men had to hide in a tobacco barn in Maryland for nearly two weeks before they could cross over to Virginia. There they were arrested by a Confederate captain. After they were released, they discovered that about half the goods they had bought had disappeared. By the time they got back to Richmond and sold the other half, they had just about broken even on the trip.

On returning home, Whitlock learned that his wife had sold off most of their tobacco stock and had made a handsome profit. He realized then tobacco would be a far better investment than running the blockade, and certainly worth more than the rapidly devaluing Confederate currency. He and his wife opened a tobacco shop at Franklin and Locust and in later years became an important tobacco merchant.

Whitlock's blockade-running escapade was a minor event, and from all evidence Jews played a relatively small role in smuggling. But the high prices for such contraband led to widespread anger among the populace, and this anger unfortunately erupted at times in efforts to make Jews the scapegoats. During the 1863 bread riots in Richmond, agitators charged that Jewish speculators had caused the shortages and were lining their own pockets at the expenses of true patriots. In a sermon preached in Fredericksburg on a Confederate fast day (27 May 1863), Michelbacher rebutted the accusations and declared flatly that "the Israelites are not speculators nor extortioners." He charged that the accusations had been "cunningly devised" to shield the real culprits. In an effort to apply logic to an emotional situation, Michelbacher pointed out that most Jewish merchants did not deal in flour, wheat, meal, corn, beef, coal, or wood, the products most subject to hoarding and profiteering. The sermon was widely reprinted both in the North and in the South.

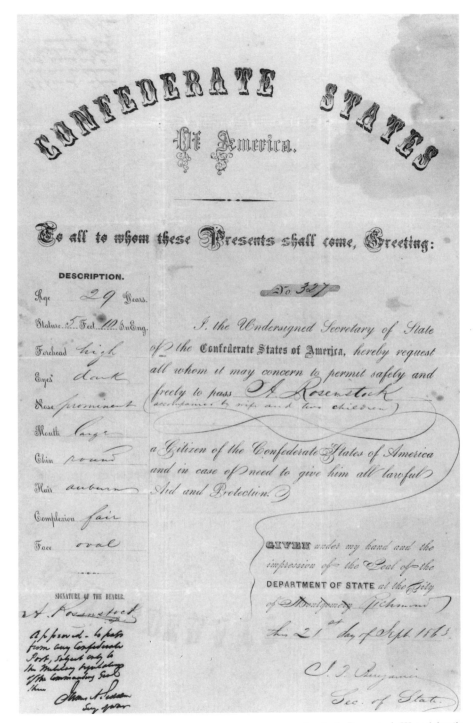

Louis A. Rosenstock III and family

In September 1863, Petersburg merchant Anthony Rosenstock was permitted to pass freely within the country or "to pass from any Confederate Port." His pass was signed by Confederate Secretary of State Judah P. Benjamin and Secretary of War James A. Seddon.

The *Richmond Examiner* often ran charges that Jews had no loyalty to the Confederacy and merely wanted to make money out of the war, primarily by providing inferior goods to the army. A cartoon, "Shoddy or the Vulture of the Camp," was popular north and south of the Mason-Dixon line, and the *Examiner* asserted that Jews "flocked as vultures to every point of gain."

Allegations by the *Examiner* led the House of Representatives to appoint a special committee in early 1864 to look into the charges. According to the paper, an unnamed member of the House had vouched for, and obtained, passports for three Jews out of the Confederate states and for this service had received $3,000.

A special committee of the House investigated and found the accusations totally baseless. The editor of the paper, John Moncure Daniel, explained to the committee that he had forbidden the publication of the story, but it had gotten into print "accidentally." Daniel's veracity is hard to accept, given the many anti-Semitic articles carried in his paper. In fact, in the same issue carrying the charge against the congressman there appeared two other items relating to Jews. One asserted that four men, three Jews and their guide, had been captured and brought back to Richmond after having attempted to cross Confederate lines into the North. The other reported that a perusal of the registers of local hotels showed that "there are numerous arrivals here of the tribe of Benjamin, who are seeking an outlet to the enemy's lines."

Although Union troops had tried to capture Richmond almost from the beginning of the war, the city withstood conquest until the end. Other sections of the state proved less fortunate. Parts of the Valley and much of northern Virginia were occupied by Federal troops through most of the war. In early 1862 northern forces under the command of Marcus M. Spiegel, a German immigrant who had settled in Ohio, occupied Woodstock. Spiegel had joined up after Fort Sumter and rose in a relatively short time to the rank of colonel of the 120th Ohio Infantry. In a letter to his wife he wrote of surprising Jews he met in towns under his jurisdiction. When he recognized a Jew, he would use a few words of Hebrew or Yiddish and then smile at their reaction. They would ask in return if he was Jewish, and upon receiving a firm yes, they would invite him and his officers to their home for dinner and do all they could to treat him with respect.

Although Jews had not lived in Alexandria as long as they had in Richmond or Norfolk, nonetheless many of the Jewish families there had strong southern sentiments, and several of the young men left the city to

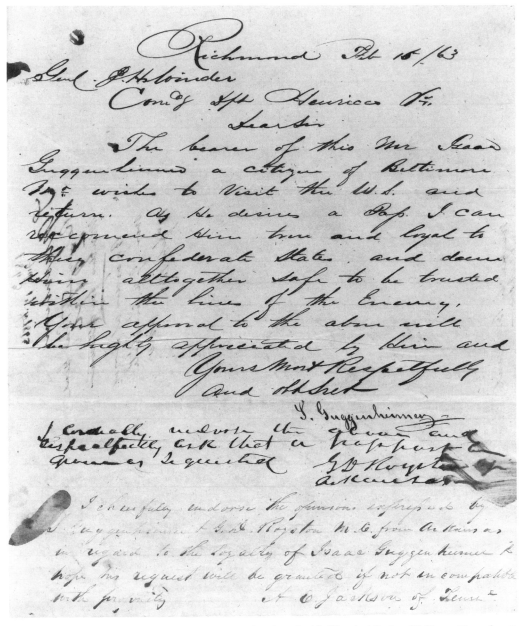

American Jewish Historical Society, Waltham, Massachusetts

In February 1863, Isaac Guggenheimer, a citizen of Baltimore, sought permission to pass through Confederate lines in order to travel to the North. Two colleagues vouched for his loyalty.

serve with the Confederate army. On the day that Virginia voted to secede from the Union, Henry Schwarz ran an advertisement in the *Alexandria Gazette*. Despite its efforts at lightheartedness, there was an underlying tone of despair that affected many of the city's residents:

The War has certainly begun.
Go to SCHWARZ's you'll see there is no fun;
He'll sell you for 25 cents the 'Panic Envelope',
Containing Hose, Handkerchiefs, Mitts, Combs, and Soap.
In others are Pocket Books, Cravats, Collars and Sleeves,
And everything that mortal can conceive;
The motto of selling so cheap,
Is simply as he needs money a heap.
As there is trouble all over the land,
He is anxious to dispose of Goods on hand;
Call and see him or send in your order,
And get the 'Panic Envelope' for only a quarter.
As for the worth of your money, you need not be mistaken.
It is as sure as Fort Sumter is taken.

Only a few weeks later, the New York Zouaves marched into Alexandria and occupied the city for the rest of the war. Those who remained found themselves subject to the indignities of occupation, and in 1863 Union officials drew up a list of Alexandria citizens, including several Jews, considered disloyal. They received an alternative of either proving their loyalty at once or facing deportation behind southern lines.

The provost marshal's records described Joseph Rosenthal and his brother Albert, who owned a shoe store on King Street, as having been "formerly connected with all rebel movements while rebs were here." The report also labeled Simon Waterman, who had lived in Virginia for at least fifteen years, as "Secesh but guarded in conversation." Waterman's wife, Caroline, also found her name on the list. The Rosenthals managed to prove their loyalty, but the Watermans could not, and only a last-minute rescission of the deportation order by the secretary of war prevented their exile. Waterman later had to sign the mandatory loyalty oath in order to continue in business.

Jews apparently were not singled out for close scrutiny and were treated equally with their neighbors. In fact, the military-controlled city council named Peter Seldner to the wartime board of health in 1863, perhaps the first Alexandria Jew to hold public office.

If Richmond escaped outright occupation, it nonetheless suffered grievously. Time and again Union armies drove toward the city. Its residents staggered under the burdens of insufficient food and wounded soldiers to nurse. In 1863 the city was the scene of bread riots as hungry men and women marched toward Capitol Square and then began looting the downtown stores, first for food and then for anything they could carry. Jefferson Davis himself helped to quell the unrest by riding into the mob on horseback and ordering troops to fire on the looters if they did not depart. In April 1865, Lee's defense line at Petersburg collapsed, and he sent a message to Davis to evacuate Richmond. Many citizens fled; others did not.

The majority of the Jews, who had clearly supported the Confederate cause, decided to remain and take their chances during the occupation.

On 2 April, the day before Union troops entered the city, Confederate officials set fire to the large stores of tobacco that had accumulated in the city to prevent their falling into enemy hands. A strong wind blew up from the south, and before long much of the downtown business district had been turned into an inferno. In her diary Emma Mordecai recalled seeing the glow of the flames and hearing one explosion after another and the concern she had for relatives and friends still in the city. Soon after, worry turned to fear as she and her sister-in-law had to deal with marauding troops and freed slaves and then the certainty of knowing that her beloved Richmond had been destroyed.

As the 4th Massachusetts Cavalry rode down Main Street, they were greeted with scowls and jeers from the bystanders, but as they approached one house, a second-floor window opened, and a handsome young woman flung to the breeze a large flag showing the Stars and Stripes. Major Atherton H. Stevens and his men wheeled in front of the house and "gave a lusty cheer for Old Glory and another for the fair woman who had gladdened their hearts." Had they known the truth of this deception, they might not have cheered so lustily.

Rachel Semon Louis and her parents had lived in Richmond during most of the war, and as the end approached, the older Semons wanted to escape before Union troops arrived. But as Louis noted, "I had $10,000 worth of tobacco in my rooms and had determined to save it. Then the idea came into my head that as soon as the troops came into town I would hoist the flag, and would be assured protection." Her father believed that she would not dare to do it, but the strong-willed woman thought she had little to lose.

She had embroidered the flag in 1859. It showed George Washington on horseback waving the Stars and Stripes while trampling the Union Jack underfoot. During the war, lest she be thought a traitor, Louis kept the flag concealed behind a mirror. The ruse worked, and although a number of surrounding houses were destroyed, the Semon residence survived intact. But the family lost the tobacco anyway, because her husband and father, fearing the Union soldiers would seize it, had hired draymen to move it to a safe warehouse, where the great fire consumed it.

And so Rachel Louis, like the other Jews of Virginia, faced the end of the war with little but her determination to begin life anew.

RESTORATION AND RENEWAL

THE end of the war found Virginia and the South in ruins—plantations devastated, cities destroyed, and the economy a shambles. Jews suffered no less and no more than did their Christian neighbors. After the peace at Appomattox, they too set about rebuilding their lives and their businesses.

They proved remarkably successful, and in the fifteen or so years after the end of hostilities Jewish communities as well as individuals in the Old Dominion reestablished themselves. Fledgling congregations felt emboldened to erect synagogues as their members regained their old positions in the local economies, and new ones arose in smaller towns.

Then in 1880 a great wave of immigration broke on American shores and profoundly affected the society as a whole as well as that of Jewish communities both North and South. Just as the Germans had reinvigorated communal life in the 1840s and 1850s, so the newcomers from eastern Europe did the same in the three decades before World War I.

Visitors to the South after the war gazed on scenes of utter devastation. In the towns, fires and other ravages of war had gutted the business districts; in the countryside, fields lay neglected, and once proud plantation houses stood in ruins. Much of the personal wealth of southerners had also been destroyed. Confederate bonds and money were worthless, little more than a painful reminder of the Lost Cause, while the emancipation of the slaves had in one blow wiped out property that had been valued at more than $2 billion. More than 258,000 Confederate soldiers had died during the war, and thousands of others had been left crippled or otherwise incapacitated by the fighting. As a result, numerous southern families faced the postwar years without adult males to help in the rebuilding, and many faced the bleak prospects of starvation and homelessness. Confederate veterans, including members of some of Richmond's most prominent families, were compelled to take jobs as simple day laborers in order to hold body and soul together.

The presence of large numbers of Union soldiers in the former capital of the Confederacy initially upset many residents, but before long they recognized that the troops had put an end to the looting and rampant criminality that had followed the fire. Moreover, the provisional governor

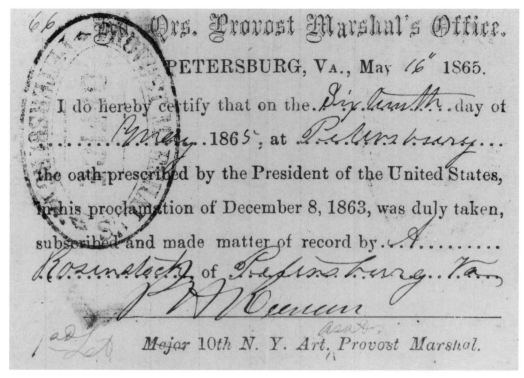

Hrs. Provost Marshal's Office,

PETERSBURG, Va., May *16ᵗ* 1865.

I do hereby certify that on the..*Sixteenth*..day of
............*May*..1865, at *Petersburg*...
the oath prescribed by the President of the United States,
in his proclamation of December 8, 1863, was duly taken,
subscribed and made matter of record by..*A.*.........
Rosenstock of *Petersburg Va.*

Major 10th N. Y. Art. Provost Marshal.

Loyalty oaths, such as the one sworn by Anthony Rosenstock of Petersburg, were required to resume business under the Reconstruction government.

of the state, Francis H. Pierpont, understood the situation far better than did many Reconstruction officials in other parts of the South. Although determined to protect the freedmen, he encouraged the white community to get on with rebuilding its lives. Policies promulgated in Washington often frustrated this generous goal, but Virginians for the most part did exactly that, so that by the time Reconstruction formally ended in 1870, the commonwealth was a far different place than it had been following the defeat of Lee's armies.

Rebekah Bettelheim, arriving in Richmond with her father in 1869, wrote of the devastation still evident: "The people had not recuperated. The war was still the chief fireside and table topic, bitterness toward the North was expressed in almost every breath. As the seat of the Confederacy, Richmond was full of memories of martial activities, of great personalities directing the government and the war machine, of war-time rationing, and want and destitution."

The entire life's labors of Jewish businessmen in Richmond, Tidewater, and the Valley had gone up in smoke, and many of them stood destitute, their stores and even some of their homes destroyed. They did the only

Virginia Historical Society

W. Harry Bagby Collection, Virginia Historical Society

In 1842 William Thalhimer, a German peddler, opened a one-room dry goods store in Richmond. By 1875, the store had relocated to 501 East Broad Street. In 1881 Gustavus, Moses, and Amelia Thalhimer (first, second, and fourth from the left) posed in front of their store for Merchants Photographic Company. During the twentieth century, the family venture expanded into a large network of department stores across Virginia and several other southern states. Changing demography and the rise of the suburban mall closed the last Thalhimers store in January 1992.

thing they could—they started over again and played a key part in helping their cities recover. Jewish merchants, like their Christian counterparts, did not start out completely empty-handed. They were no longer newcomers to the area but had put roots down. They and their stores had reputations; they had neighbors who had been loyal customers before the war and who would return as their finances improved. For some merchants at least, connections made before the war could be used to help get back on their feet.

William Thalhimer knew he could expect no assistance from his fellow Richmonders. Even if they wanted to help, they had nothing to offer. Their stores, like his, had been destroyed in the fire, and had courts been functioning normally, most of the city's merchants would have been forced to declare bankruptcy. Thalhimer went to New York, where he called on businessmen he had known personally before the war, and they agreed to give him a line of credit based on nothing more than their knowledge of him as an honest man. On his way back to Richmond, he stopped in Baltimore, and there two more friends agreed to extend credit. His good name had earned him the financing he needed to begin business anew.

While some merchants were buoyed by the good faith and credit of prewar associates, others relied on new opportunities and developing markets to forge their future. Tobacco had always been an important cash crop for Virginia, but after the war the combination of improved manufacturing techniques and the expansion of markets moved tobacco from farm product to industry in the state. Philip Whitlock, who had made a daring, if unprofitable, trip through the Union blockade, successfully positioned himself to take advantage of this opportunity. Thanks to a happenstance meeting with a skilled cigar maker in his dry goods shop in Richmond, Whitlock learned to roll his own cigars and began selling his handiwork at his counter. The cigars were well received, and he soon began hiring labor, typically young women, to increase production. The eventual result was the construction of a five-story factory at Twentieth and Franklin in 1886. The key to Whitlock's success was affordability and packaging: Old Virginia Cheroots were economically priced at five for 10 cents, and the featured trademark of a black servant guaranteed product recognition. (The likeness on the package was that of Barbour Graves, a family employee who always wore his brass spectacles atop his head but never actually used them.)

By 1889, the P. Whitlock Old Virginia Cheroot & Cigar Factory was producing thirty-three million cigarettes a year, and by 1891, the company had attracted the attention of the American Tobacco Company. With Major Lewis Ginter acting for American Tobacco, Whitlock agreed to a "certain price" for his business and also to stay on for three years to run the factory. Although Whitlock never mentioned that "certain price" in his handwritten memoirs, he did underline, with the pride of an immigrant

Philip Whitlock's five-story cheroot and cigar factory in Richmond turned out 100,000 tobacco products daily and employed 300.

tailor from Poland, that his *"fortune was then realized."* Whitlock retired from the tobacco business in 1895 but continued to be active in the economic life of the city as a director for both the Savings Bank of Richmond and the Virginia Trust Company. He was vice-president of Beth Ahabah and maintained a role as a leading citizen of Richmond until his death in 1919.

Not all the merchants had the contacts or the reputation of Thalhimer or Whitlock. For some of them, the postwar years meant starting from scratch. They were aided by a development that in the end impeded rather than advanced progress in the South. With the plantation economy ruined, wholesale merchants and the men who built and owned the new railroads decided to adapt the general store, an institution well known on the frontier, to the more established but devastated southern states. The general store specialized in the materials farmers needed—feed, farm implements, fertilizer, food—and only incidentally carried the dry goods that constituted the heart of the urban stores.

Because the farmers had no money with which to pay for these items—yet needed them in order to plant and harvest their crops—the wholesalers devised a credit scheme tied to the land and the crops. The store would extend credit to the farmer and in return take a mortgage on his harvest. The stores in addition served as post offices and also provided anything else the farmers needed, which could be charged against the crop lien. Once a farmer had signed the agreement, he could not get credit anywhere else and thus had to pay whatever prices the store owner charged.

In a few places Jews ran these general stores, but for the most part they provided the only competition the credit stores faced. The Jews opened cash stores, where farmers who had some money—even a little—could escape the extortionate rates of the general stores. If they extended credit, they usually established some sort of a buying-on-time plan. One writer has attributed the success of these small cash stores to two character traits of their Jewish owners. First, the Jewish merchants had infinite patience in dealing with people in small business affairs, and second, they were willing to bargain over prices.

Another aspect of Reconstruction Virginia was the return of the backpack and wagon peddlers, who served the more rural areas and the black population as well, and who sold everything from needles, thread, and fabric to small household utensils. This period did not last long, because these Jewish peddlers, like the ones who had gone out in the 1840s, also wanted to settle down. During Reconstruction, however, they played an important part in the rural economy of Virginia.

Across the state in Norfolk and Petersburg, in Alexandria and Charlottesville, in Fredericksburg and Staunton, other merchants began to rebuild their lives and businesses. *The Owl*, a Jewish publication in New Orleans, smilingly noted that the war must have produced an Americanizing effect on the Jews of Norfolk and especially on its leading family, the Hofheimers, who from this point on began to name their male children after patriotic Americans. In Danville, Julius Kaufman opened a men's clothing store on Main Street that became a fixture for the next ninety-two years. Kaufman himself became a leading figure on the city's common council. And just as merchants restarted their businesses, so Jewish communities also began to rebuild.

One sign of the optimism of the community was that almost immediately after the surrender at Appomattox, the new fraternal order of B'nai B'rith opened chapters in the South. The organization had been founded in New York in 1843, with the aim of promoting Judaism in the New World and providing aid for Jews in need. Through most of the rest of the nineteenth century, the membership consisted almost entirely of German Jews, but this composition changed about World War I, when the society began to welcome the eastern Europeans and their children. By 1897, when the national organization counted some 15,000 members, the movement established B'nai B'rith Women, which soon had chapters throughout the country and overseas.

The first Virginia chapters appear to have been established in Richmond in 1865, and the split between the Reform-minded Germans and the

TO THE ISRAELITES OF THE SOUTH.

Richmond, Va. June 5th, 1833.

While the world yet rings with the narrative of a brave people's struggle for independence, and while the story of the hardships so nobly endured for Liberty's sake is yet a theme but half exhausted, the countless graves of the myriads of heroes who spilled their noble blood in defence of that glorious cause, lie neglected, not alone unmarked by tablet or sculptured urn, but literally vanishing before the relentless finger of Time. Within the past four weeks, there have been formed by the ladies of Richmond two Associations, viz: the "Hollywood" and the "Oakwood," having for their object the care and renovation of the soldiers' graves in those cemeteries.

Cotemporaneously with the above, we, the Hebrew Ladies, formed a similar Association, with the view of caring for the graves of Jewish soldiers; which, of course, would not be embraced in the work of either of the first named Societies.

In our own cemetery repose, alas! the sacred remains of many a loved brother, son and husband, to whose relatives, in the far sunny South, it would be a solace to know that the pious duty of preserving from decay the last resting place of their lost ones, although denied to them to perform, is yet sacredly fulfilled by the members of the "Hebrew Ladies' Memorial Association."

It is our intention to mound and turf each grave, and to place at the head of each a simple stone, inscribed with the name, State, and time and place of death; subsequently, to rear a monument commemorative of their brave deeds.

In order, however, to successfully accomplish our object, we need some pecuniary assistance. Our scant and somewhat needy community, already so heavily taxed, has done well; but we find "this work is too great for us:" therefore, with a full confidence in the sympathy and co-operation of our people elsewhere, we make this appeal for aid, well knowing that as Israelites and true patriots, they will not refuse to assist in rearing a monument which shall serve not only to commemorate the bravery of our dead, but the gratitude and admiration of the living, for those who so nobly perished in what we deemed a just and righteous cause; and while as Israelites we mourn the untimely loss of our loved ones, it will be a grateful reflection that they suffered not their country to call in vain.

In time to come, when our grief shall have become, in a measure, silenced, and when the malicious tongue of slander, ever so ready to assail Israel, shall be raised against us, then, with a feeling of mournful pride, will we point to this monument and say: "There is our reply."

MRS. ABRAHAM LEVY.
Corresponding Secretary of the Hebrew Ladies' Memorial Association.

Beth Ahabah Museum and Archives

In 1866 Rachel Levy issued an appeal for funds for the Hebrew Ladies' Memorial Association to mark graves in the Confederate plot of the Hebrew Cemetery in Richmond.

more traditional members of the community led to the creation of two chapters. Rimmon Lodge No. 68 consisted primarily of members of Beth Ahabah, while Benjamin Lodge No. 69 catered mainly to Beth Shalome and the Orthodox Kenesseth Israel. A few years later a third branch, Paradise Lodge No. 223, emerged, and not until 1905 did the three lodges consolidate as one. Although Jews continued to be active in Masonry, the establishment of a completely Jewish fraternal order had great appeal. The vigor of Richmond Jews in behalf of B'nai B'rith led the national leaders to schedule their annual convention in Richmond in 1890.

In Harrisonburg the close of the war saw new immigrants joining the Jews already there, and despite the economic devastation of the war, they felt sufficiently confident by 1867 to establish a congregation and to undertake building a synagogue. In Norfolk that same year, Congregation Ohef Sholom leased a building for $500 a year, a significant sum during the Reconstruction era. In Richmond the organization of Beth Israel in 1866 gave the city four congregations for a time.

Perhaps no community underwent as much of a transformation in the immediate postwar years as did Alexandria. Martial law had been in effect since the early days of the war, and many Jewish merchants had ceased business rather than take an oath of allegiance to the Union government. But the city's importance as a major military base and the large number of troops stationed there attracted many Jews loyal to the Union from northern cities such as Baltimore, Philadelphia, New York, and, of course, Washington. In addition, some southern Jews who had opposed secession also came to the city. David Bendheim closed his business in Lynchburg and joined his brother in Alexandria, while a fair number of Jews made their way from Norfolk. In 1859 the estimated Jewish population of the city had been fifty; by the end of the war, it had risen to between three and four hundred.

King Street, which had been practically deserted in the early days of the war, took on a new life, and most of the stores in the business district operated under Jewish names. In fact, the local newspaper commented in September 1862 that the closing of so many stores on King Street for the Jewish holidays "gave the town quite a dull appearance yesterday." Similar comments could be found each of the next four years.

After the war, some of the immigrants went back home—the Reizensteins returned to Front Royal, the Hofheimers and others to Norfolk, and the Hechts to Baltimore. Meyer Kaufman moved his store across the Potomac to Washington. As a result, Alexandria underwent a slow but steady erosion of its Jewish population. By the turn of the century, only a little more than one hundred Jews lived there. Nonetheless, in the decade after Appomattox, Alexandria Jewry enjoyed vigorous and exciting times. After the wartime restrictions, social life expanded. Many balls and parties merited newspaper attention. The community established a German school, and in 1871 Beth El built a synagogue on Washington Street north of historic Christ Church, one it used for the next eighty-four years. This was the first synagogue constructed in the Washington metropolitan area specifically for a Reform congregation.

No one epitomized the Alexandria community more than Henry Strauss, the owner of a clothing store on King Street and for more than

Beth El Hebrew Congregation Archives, Alexandria

Sarepta Hall on King Street in Alexandria had the department store of Samuel Rosenberg (1879–1930) on the first floor. Congregation Agudas Achim met on an upper floor in the early twentieth century.

thirty years a central figure in the city's political as well as its Jewish life. Strauss had emigrated from Germany in 1848 as a teenager, and his family, after passing briefly through Alexandria, had settled in Georgia. Too short to serve in the regular army, he volunteered for the Home Guard, and after the state was overrrun by Union forces, young Strauss was jailed for his open hostility to the North. He made his way to Alexandria, where he married and joined a variety of communal activities, including the Pioneer Baseball Club and one of the volunteer fire departments.

In 1877 he won his first elected office, a seat on the board of aldermen, and he was heavily involved in city politics until his death thirty-one years later. Strauss ran for mayor in the Democratic primary of 1889, and following the conventions of the time, he opened his purse liberally. A steady stream of customers visited his clothing store, and the following is typical of many conversations that day: "Mr. Strauss, I'd like you to meet Mr. Brown. I'm taking him down to the polls and I'm sure that he's going to vote for you, but he surely will need a pair of overshoes to get there." By the end of the day, Strauss found his stock depleted, but he had still lost the election. Although Strauss announced in disgust that he was retiring from politics, he did not do so, and in 1891, on his third try, he won election as Alexandria's mayor; two years later he ran unopposed for reelection.

The growth of Jewish communities also introduced strife in several cities, where congregations split over the question of adopting the Reform rituals. In 1866 Maximilian J. Michelbacher introduced the confirmation ceremony at Beth Ahabah in Richmond and accelerated that synagogue's march toward full adoption of Reform. In Norfolk, members of Ohef Sholom debated seriously and often angrily about proposed reforms. When the committee on ritual brought in its report in December 1869 recommending the adoption of the Reform *minhag*, a number of members resigned in protest and established a new congregation. In Alexandria, those Jews dissatisfied with the adoption of Reform at Beth El went across the river and joined the Washington Hebrew Congregation.

Why did the adoption of Reform cause such strife, and what did it mean? Although the issue split many Jewish communities, a comparison to the Protestant Reformation is misleading. Martin Luther's theses shattered the universal church, because for a thousand years nearly all Christians in the West had offered their allegiance to the pope, the Catholic church, and its doctrines. There had never been a "church universal" in Judaism. Although traditional Jews subscribed to a theology that had not changed much since the third or fourth century C.E., there was no chief rabbi or *sanhedrin* (council) that spoke authoritatively on religious doctrine or practice. Even in those European countries that had chief rabbis, these leaders' positions were more ceremonial than doctrinal. Ever since the destruction of the Temple in Jerusalem in 70 C.E. and the creation of the local synagogue a century or two later, Judaism had been a decentralized religion. Each congregation governed itself and subscribed to Jewish ritual and laws handed down from the Talmudic time.

Reform offered the first serious challenge to this theology. Although the movement began in Germany, its greatest growth came in the United States. The founders of Reform wanted to make Judaism more modern, partly in its theology but primarily in its ritual. Theologically Reform abandoned the dream and the prayer that Jews be returned and reestablished as a people in Palestine, did away with many of the laws of *kashruth* (which governed what Jews could eat), relaxed the restrictions on Sabbath observance, and most important of all, denied the identification of Israel as a people with the Torah. This last change is what upset traditionalists the

Ohef Sholom Temple, Norfolk

Congregation Ohef Sholom in Norfolk welcomed a new member on 24 May 1901, when
Blanche B. Metzger was confirmed.

When Rebecca Michelbacher, the daughter of Maximilian J. Michelbacher, married David Mitteldorfer in 1869, her father's congregation presented her a silver samovar. Tragically, she died less than a year later.

Courtesy of Richard Bendheim

Beth Ahabah Museum and Archives

Her widower, David, and his brother, Ellis, ran a dry goods store in Richmond on East Broad Street, three blocks up from the Thalhimers' store. Mitteldorfer's advertised a clearance sale about 1910.

most, because it did away with the extensive and complex set of rules that governed everyday communal and individual life.

The Reformers responded in part to what they saw as the need to modernize Judaism and in part to the necessities of the time. Emancipation in Europe and the freedom of the United States did away with the external pressures that had kept Jews tied to the local communities. Men and women would remain Jewish only if they believed in the tenets of the religion and felt comfortable in its practice.

The impetus for Reform in America came primarily from the laity, because there were so few trained rabbis in the country. In Virginia, for example, only a few congregations had full-time rabbis as late as the 1880s. Michelbacher, for instance, although he served as spiritual head of Beth Ahabah for three decades, had no formal training as a rabbi and was, in fact, known primarily as a teacher. Most congregations used lay readers to lead services, and these men had few qualifications other than their ability to read Hebrew. As a result, as congregations demanded more "modern" services, the Reformers ran into no opposition from rabbis, although they often had to fight bitterly with other members of the congregation who wanted to maintain traditional practices. Perhaps as much as anything, the laity wanted more dignified services, ones that frankly resembled those of their Protestant neighbors in which families sat and prayed together and in which music played a large role in the ritual.

Eventually, thanks in large measure to the work of Isaac Mayer Wise, a seminary for training American Reform rabbis was established in the Hebrew Union College at Cincinnati, and shortly afterward national organizations of Reform congregations (the Union of American Hebrew Congregations) and of Reform rabbis (the Central Conference of American Rabbis) came into being.

The most important impetus to the rise of Reform did not lie in a rejection of traditional Judaism; in its core aspects—monotheism and ethics—Reform adopted the basic teachings, although it did reject the important notion of Israel as a unique people tied to the Torah and commanded to obey its laws. More than anything else, American Jews in the latter nineteenth century wanted to be accepted fully in this country and were willing to shed those ritualistic aspects of their religion that set them apart.

Nowhere else did they succeed quite as effectively as they did in the South, where Christians often referred to the synagogue as "the Jewish church." By the 1870s, there were Reform congregations in the larger cities of the commonwealth and in some of the smaller ones as well. There were no overnight conversions, because for the most part the laity felt its way slowly. In Virginia one did not find an Isaac Mayer Wise or a David Einhorn, but then neither did one find an outstanding traditionalist such as

Isaac Leeser, who opposed Reform but who had left Richmond years earlier. Congregations became Reform step by very careful step, often keeping elements of the old traditional ritual while introducing the new *minhag.*

Beth Ahabah is a good case in point. There had been agitation from the laity for a number of years to introduce some reforms but never to abandon the old rituals entirely. Maximilian Michelbacher took a few steps along the road by initiating confirmation services after the war and teaching a Sunday religious school. Although Michelbacher stayed with Beth Ahabah until his death in 1879, the congregation brought in a trained rabbi, Albert S. Bettelheim, who stayed in Richmond from 1869 to 1874. He cautiously initiated a number of reforms and has been described as a "right-wing reformer," probably the only kind who could have succeeded in Richmond. Small but important things, such as the ending of the practice of kissing the *zizit* (the fringes of the *talit,* or prayer shawl) and the elimination of the reading of a section of the Prophets on the Sabbath, marked his tenure. But he opposed suggestions from his board that he go further, and then the tragic death of his wife led him to leave Richmond. In the end, Bettelheim joined the so-called Historical School and became a founder of the Conservative movement, located between Reform and tradition, but much closer to the latter.

Bettelheim was a learned man, and he quickly struck up a friendship with the Catholic bishop of the city, James Gibbons, later Cardinal Gibbons. The intellectual discussions the two men had and the friendship they enjoyed was a hallmark of relations between the Reform rabbis of Beth Ahabah and the leading Christian ministers of the city, a tradition expanded during the long tenure of Edward N. Calisch and carried down to the present in the work of Jack D. Spiro. These relationships, which the congregation's boards heartily encouraged, grew out of that determination to be "just like the Christians" in all but theology. The acceptance of their rabbis as part of the city's clergy gave a legitimacy to the Reformers and certainly made them feel more "American."

During Bettelheim's stay in Richmond, a prod to reforming existed in a breakaway congregation, Beth Israel, led by William Flegenheimer and others who wanted to embrace the new Reform mold completely and more rapidly than did the membership of Beth Ahabah. The lack of a strong financial base caused Beth Israel to rejoin the parent congregation in 1871, but the return of these more outspoken Reformers pushed Beth Ahabah even further away from traditionalism. Reform took a few more steps during the brief two-year tenure of Abraham Hoffman of Baltimore, during which the congregation abandoned the old traditional prayer book and adopted the modernized *Abodat Israel.* Beth Ahabah also joined the Union of American Hebrew Congregations in 1875, only two years after that organization's founding, and thus publicly aligned itself with the Reform movement, even if it had still not adopted all of the movement's practices.

The next rabbi, Abraham Harris, had been a professor at the new Hebrew Union College before coming to Richmond, but he, too, would have to be classified as a conservative reformer, willing to modernize the ritual but only cautiously. He was the congregation's first rabbi who spoke English rather than German as his native tongue, and like Michelbacher, he proved to be very popular with his congregants. He joined the congregation at a time of rapid growth, and in 1880 Beth Ahabah built a new and larger synagogue on North Eleventh Street between Clay and Marshall, on the same site as its earlier building. Under Harris's leadership, Friday evening family services began, which soon came to be as important as the normal Saturday morning gatherings. Harris served thirteen years and then, shortly after delivering his sermon on 24 January 1891, was stricken and died in the pulpit.

His successor, the energetic and charismatic Edward Nathan Calisch, served as Beth Ahabah's rabbi from 1891 to 1945 and made it one of the premier Reform congregations in the country. Under Calisch, Beth Ahabah did away with skullcaps during services, adopted a more Reform prayer book and hymnal, and aligned itself fully with the liberal rather than the conservative wing of the movement.

Calisch presided not only over the ritual transformation of Beth Ahabah but physical changes as well. In 1898 Beth Shalome, which had been barely viable for the previous two decades, merged with Beth Ahabah, which later took as its founding date 1789. In 1904 the congregation built and consecrated its new synagogue, the cathedral-like structure on West Franklin Street, which it still uses today. The edifice achieved the congregation's desire that it have a noble and handsome house of worship.

In Alexandria, Beth El also affiliated with the Union of American Hebrew Congregations in 1883. The impetus for this action came from the fact that starting that year, the congregation had no full-time rabbi until 1939. Instead, a series of student rabbis from the Hebrew Union College came to conduct holiday services. The first of these rabbis, Morris Sachs, proved extremely energetic and besides convincing the congregation to join the UAHC also organized the Ladies Educational Aid Society of Alexandria to provide assistance for poor HUC students.

The emergence of Reform as the dominant strain of Judaism in Virginia and elsewhere by the 1880s attests to the desire for Americanization that the German immigrants possessed. The United States was a land of freedom, a new land, and while they did not want to abandon their religion, they did want to make it compatible with what they saw as modern conditions. In Alexandria, Harrisonburg, Norfolk, and elsewhere, the German Jews and their children had cause to give thanks to America. The memories of the Civil War remained for many decades, but the Old Dominion had recovered its former prosperity. Despite an ill-advised and futile effort to declare the United States a "Christian country," most Virginians recognized that their Jewish neighbors had stood and fought with them during the war and had suffered alongside them afterward. The desire of the immigrants to become Americanized seemed to have come true in Virginia and in other parts of the United States as well. And then came the eastern Europeans.

In 1880 Count Constantine Pobyedonostzev, the chief adviser to Tsar Alexander II, devised a simple scheme to rid Mother Russia of its Jews—one-third would accept baptism, one-third would starve to death, and one-third would emigrate. Soon the government promulgated dozens of laws to make this harsh policy a reality, and Pobyedonostzev saw at least part of his dream fulfilled. Between 1880 and the closing of free immigration in 1925, more than 2.5 million Jews, about one-third of the Jewish population of eastern Europe, came to America.

Unlike the earlier Sephardic and German immigrants, many of whom tended to come from a *petit bourgeois* background, the eastern Europeans were overwhelmingly poor and carried on their backs their small trove of

Beth Ahabah Museum and Archives

Rabbi Edward Nathan Calisch (1865–1946) of Beth Ahabah in Richmond (fifth from the right) posed with President William Howard Taft (center) at the White House in 1915 following the Richmonder's address at George Washington's tomb. The reform-minded Calisch served as rabbi of Beth Ahabah from 1891 through 1945.

possessions—bedding, kitchen utensils, and the ubiquitous samovar. At Hamburg or Bremen they paid dearly for the right to sail three weeks in the steerage holds, jammed into inadequate space that soon stank from a lack of fresh air and insufficient sanitary facilities. According to one of the popular immigrant guides of the day, the passage constituted "a kind of hell that cleanses a man of his sins before coming to Columbus' land." Whatever its spiritual values, few who made the crossing ever forgot its horrors.

Once in the United States, the newcomers labored to earn a living and to save enough money to bring over wives, children, parents, and other relatives. The railroads and mail-order houses by this time had begun to deprive peddlers of their role in the rural distribution of goods, thus closing off an avenue that had been followed so successfully by the Germans. But new factories catering to urban markets needed workers, and so the immigrants for the most part crowded into northern cities, or when they came south, also looked for opportunity in the cities rather than the countryside. In Virginia the Jewish population rose from 2,500 in 1880 to more than 15,000 twenty years later, a proportional growth far greater than that following the German migration a generation earlier.

In Virginia and elsewhere a social cleavage quickly opened between the older German Jewish communities and the newcomers, although there are many instances of the Germans trying to make the eastern Europeans welcome. But as late as the 1940s, a marriage between a daughter of the Reform German community and a son of the Orthodox Russian congregation in Richmond was considered an intermarriage. In general, the attitude of the *yahudim* (the German Jews) toward the *yidden* (eastern European Jews) resembled the same patronization with which the Germans had been greeted when they had arrived.

What the established community feared above all was that the new immigration would undo all that they had worked so hard to achieve. Both in the North and South, German Jewish leaders doubted that this human flood would ever amount to anything. "Those people" seemed barbaric vestiges of the Middle Ages, unsuited for American democracy. "The thoroughly acclimated American Jew," according to the *Hebrew Standard*, "has no religious, social or intellectual sympathies with them. He is closer to the Christian sentiment around him than to the Judaism of these miserable darkened Hebrews." The New York correspondent of the *American Israelite*, after a visit to Ward's Island, reported: "They look exactly like the Polish riff-raff of which most European cities are only too familiar.... And what is said by those who know of their personal characteristics is not calculated to increase the sympathy which we are all bound to feel for them."

For those already established in America, the influx of Russian Jews presented a quandary. They recognized a Jewish kinship with the newcom-

Courtesy of Lois Sandler Graboyes

In 1913 Ben Sandler, who had emigrated from Latvia, received naturalization papers in Key West. Two years later, he moved to Petersburg.

ers, however distant it might be, and thousands of the new immigrants benefited from the various philanthropic agencies established by the German community. Moreover, the forces of persecution in Russia that had triggered this new migration bore more than a faint resemblance to the anti-Semitism that had propelled them and their parents to leave central Europe four decades earlier.

The differences between the German and Russian communities centered on both cultural and religious matters. By 1880, Reform had become the dominant strand of religion in the United States, but the newcomers overwhelmingly adhered to traditional or, as it would now be called, Orthodox practices. They dressed differently, and until they had spent some time in America, clung to the apparel of eastern Europe, long coats for the men, head scarves for the women, garments that quite obviously set them apart. Moreover, whereas the German migration had fanned out through-out the country, the Russians settled in the cities, turning places like New York's lower East Side into one of the world's largest ghettos.

Would these people ever assimilate? And if not, how would Christian America treat not only the newcomers, but the older, established Jews as well? The United States had been blessedly free of the anti-Semitism that had characterized European society for centuries. Would the arrival of these new Jews—and so many of them—trigger hatred of the Jews in this country?

Unfortunately, anti-Semitism did increase in the latter part of the nineteenth century, although it is hard to tell how much of it derived from the Civil War and how much from the new immigration. Patterns of social exclusion accelerated in the last quarter of the century and did not change significantly until after World War II. In 1877 the Grand Hotel in Saratoga, New York, turned away the eminent banker Joseph Seligman, a policy soon adopted by other fashionable hotels, resorts, clubs, and schools. The *Social Register* closed its list to Jews, and in 1892 the Union League Club blackballed Theodore Seligman, son of one of its founders.

The South followed suit. Between 1874 and 1890, German Jews were deeply involved in Atlanta's civic and political life, but between 1890 and 1930, only one person of Jewish descent was elected to office there, and he had long given up any attachment to or identification with Judaism. By the early twentieth century, Atlanta's most prestigious clubs no longer accepted Jews, and about the same time Richmond's elite clubs also excluded Jews, as did the Mardi Gras festivities in New Orleans. The Commonwealth Club in Richmond closed its doors to Jews despite the fact that E. T. D. Myers had been one of its founders.

Uncomplimentary references to Jews began appearing in the Richmond press, and although a Jew served as president of the Westmoreland Club in the 1880s, a sharp line had been drawn by the turn of the century. In 1916 the Reverend Edward L. Pell castigated his fellow Christians in the city, especially the women, when he asked: "I should like . . . to know what is in the heart of this Christian woman that prompts her at the moment she enters a social club to turn and slam the door in the face of the sister of her Christ?" The Germans believed that the Russians had caused this new anti-Semitism; the Russians countered that the Germans had been deceiving themselves about their acceptance into American society and about how assimilated they had become.

By contrast, William Lovenstein, whose parents were German immi-grants, had been elected to the Virginia House of Delegates only four years after Appomattox and served in the assembly for almost three decades. In 1881 he ran for and was elected to the state Senate and served as its president *pro tem* in 1895–96. When he and his wife celebrated their thirtieth wedding anniversary in 1893, their guest list included many of Richmond's most prominent Christian families. On the local level during this period, Jews held a number of municipal offices throughout the state, and James B. Angle, a veteran of the Civil War, served as captain of Richmond's police force for many years.

There is no doubt that prejudice increased during these decades, but what caused this rise in anti-Semitism is open to debate. The presence of a new and very different type of immigrant has always triggered nativist sentiment, whether that group be Irish Catholic or Russian Jew in the nineteenth century or Hispanic and Asian in the twentieth. Another source of prejudice is rapid social and economic change, and the industrialization of the United States in the decades after the Civil War put enormous strains on society. The Populist and Progressive movements beginning in the 1890s responded to the problems generated by industrialization, and both movements had heavy overtones of nativism as well as racism.

In Virginia as a whole, racism easily outweighed anti-Semitism, and a number of commentators have noted that southern white Protestants who feared blacks and hated Catholics had little energy or need to focus a great deal of attention on Jews. During this period Virginia and other southern states were busily implementing the apartheid apparatus known as Jim Crow. One should not ignore the fact that anti-Semitism existed in the Old Dominion, but compared to its manifestations in the North, it appeared relatively weak. One example is that as the children of the eastern European immigrants prepared to go to college in the early twentieth century—an opportunity all but closed to Jews in Russia—some northern schools, most notably Harvard, attempted to impose a quota on the number of Jewish students admitted. One result is that bright Jewish students began looking for alternatives where they could get a good education, such as the University of Virginia. Jews, especially those from New York, began applying in ever greater numbers until in 1926–27 they constituted 8.5 percent of the student body and, in the words of the university's historian, "were usually among the ablest scholars in the institution."

Although some within Mr. Jefferson's university greeted the arrival of bright students, others found their religion troublesome. The dean of the college wrote to President Edwin A. Alderman suggesting that the university "place some limits" on the admission of Jews because he expected "their numbers to grow rapidly hereafter as the Jews are beginning to find out they are well treated here." Fortunately, Alderman chose not to act.

Because so many of the new immigrants settled in the cities, some Jewish philanthropies believed that if a significant number of the newcomers could be diverted to farming and to settling outside the eastern metropolitan centers, it might reduce anti-Jewish sentiment. Under the leadership of the Baron de Hirsch Fund, some two dozen Jewish agricultural colonies were established in various parts of the country. In 1882 thirty families founded a colony on Sicily Island, Louisiana, only to be wiped out soon afterward by a flood. In South Dakota, Jews attempted to make a go of it in Crimea and nearby Bethlehem of Judea, but after less than three years they capitulated to hailstorms, diseased crops, drought, and prairie fires. Of all the settlements, only the four in New Jersey—Alliance, Carmel, Woodbine, and Rosenhayn—survived and prospered, in no small measure because New York City offered a large nearby market for their produce.

In Virginia an abortive attempt to establish a Jewish agricultural settlement took place in Waterview on the Rappahannock River, not far from the Chesapeake Bay, a site not easily accessible from Baltimore, Washington, or Richmond. The impetus came from Joseph Friedenwald of Baltimore, who in 1882 purchased a 5,000-acre farm in Waterview. He himself came by boat with the would-be settlers, and in the first week they constructed stables for their animals as well as baking ovens. The plows and other farm implements that had been ordered had not yet arrived, but borrowing from their neighbors, they managed to plant some forty acres of rye.

Friedenwald waxed eloquently about what this opportunity meant for the newcomers: "The children will attend the public schools, and in the near future, instead of being Russian refugees, they will attach themselves to the F[irst] F[amilies of] V[irginia]." But Waterview failed, as did most of the other agricultural experiments. The Jews who were taken there, with the best of intentions by their sponsors, had been urban dwellers in the Old Country and had not the slightest idea how to farm.

———

In the urban areas of the state they prospered. In Richmond the Jewish population doubled in the last two decades of the century, and as early as 1886 the Russian Jews, who had initially affiliated with the Orthodox but Polish Kenesseth Israel, formed their own synagogue, the Sir Moses Montefiore Congregation, named for the great Anglo-Jewish philanthropist who had recently died. Within five years they purchased the property and sanctuary of Beth Shalome on Mayo Street. Speakers at the dedication ceremony included Mayor J. Taylor Ellyson, Dr. Charles H. Cory of the Richmond Theological Institute, and Julius Straus of Beth Ahabah, who urged the newcomers not to abandon the precepts of their religion.

Virginia's cities lacked the factories that marked the northern urban landscape, but they nonetheless still offered economic opportunity. In some

Peninsula Jewish Historical Society; gift of Jane Penn Clark

Jacob Brenner, a Russian émigré, established a barber shop on Jefferson Street in Newport News in 1898.

instances, the stories of the eastern Europeans are very much like that of the Germans who preceded them. Louis Zuckerman (who later owned and operated a large scrap iron and metal business) and his father came to Winchester in 1905, and they initially earned their livelihood by peddling, the same trade that the older man had pursued around Carditz, a small town in the Ukraine. When they arrived, they found seven Jewish families in the area, the oldest—the Hables—having arrived in 1872. Eventually more moved in, but the community did not have more than sixty or seventy people until after World War II and did not build a synagogue until 1954.

In Staunton the community also grew after the war, and the early 1880s found both German and eastern European Jewry arriving in the town. In 1882 L. G. Strauss, a native of South Carolina who had spent a year teaching in a small town in Texas, wanted a change of place and vocation. He noted an advertisement in a trade magazine, applied for the job, and got it—a clerk in Joseph Barth's clothing store in Staunton. Barth wisely went down to the railroad station to meet his new clerk and there found the owner of a rival clothing store who tried by every means to hire Strauss for himself. A man of his word, Strauss went with Barth and several years later married one of Barth's sisters.

A few years after this incident, another young man got off a train from Baltimore and walked north on Augusta Street until he found the chief of police, whom he recognized by his badge. He asked the officer where he might find a vacant shop, because he wanted to open a clothing store. The chief replied, "Mister, there's a train back to Baltimore tonight and you better take it. You couldn't do any business here; Mr. Barth has all the men's trade tied up throughout this area." Nonetheless, Abraham Weinberg stayed, opened the Weinberg Clothing Company, and a few years later married another of Joseph Barth's sisters. In 1911 the two companies merged as Barth, Weinberg and Company, which still does business in Staunton, although the store is no longer owned by the family. Between the coming of Strauss and World War I, a number of migrants found Staunton a pleasant place, opened businesses there, and settled down.

In Alexandria, where the Jewish population began to decline in the 1880s, the arrival of a relatively small number of Russian Jews between 1898 and 1917 helped revive the community. Very few of them came directly to Alexandria, which was not a major entrepôt for immigrants as was Boston, New York, Philadelphia, or Baltimore. As late as the turn of the century, a number of these Russians started out as peddlers, and the area they covered included much of rural Virginia and North Carolina. Like those who had gone this route before, as soon as they had accumulated sufficient capital, they settled down in an urban area and opened a store. Joseph Hayman, probably the first Russian Jew to settle permanently in Alexandria, opened a shoe store in 1902 and later expanded it to include women's clothing; the family enterprise operated the business until 1992.

In Alexandria and most of the other small towns and cities of Virginia, Russian Jews lacked the cultural infrastructure that existed in the large ethnic enclaves of New York, Boston, and other northern cities. In many ways these support systems helped newcomers adjust to life in America, but they also insulated the immigrants from having to make too rapid an adjustment. On the lower East Side of New York, for instance, one did not have to speak English with one's neighbors, employers, or even municipal officials. Everyone spoke Yiddish—the neighbors and the employers for certain—while the bright newcomers Tammany Hall recruited to its ranks served as intermediaries between the immigrants and the bureaucracy. Often the children learned to speak English in schools well before their parents had mastered even the rudiments of the language.

In the South, and certainly in Virginia, one does not find such enclaves. It is true that the Germans in the Valley and Richmond continued to speak German well after their arrival, but even they learned and spoke English because it was the language of their neighbors and the government.

Newcomers from Russia had to Americanize fairly quickly. Moreover, if they were traditional Jews, they soon discovered that the community did not provide many of the facilities they took for granted in the Old Country, such as a *mikva* (ritual bath), a *yeshiva*, where young boys learned Hebrew and the logic of the Talmud, a kosher butcher, perhaps not even a ritually acceptable cemetery.

After leaving Russia, Molly Koffler had spent some time in Baltimore, which had a large Jewish community, and she was unprepared for the sights and sounds of Alexandria, especially the Salvation Army band playing under her hotel window in lower King Street. Because she and her fellow Russians had grown up in an Orthodox setting, the Reform services of Beth El astounded them as well. Moreover, although the German Jews tried to be welcoming, they had difficulty adjusting to the newcomers. A descendant of one of the early members of Beth El recalled the differences between the two groups "were like the differences between Buddhists and Christians." Although individual Russians might be "very well accepted," there was little social intercourse between the two groups. The Russians found some of the Germans patronizing and disdainful. When some of the Russian women accepted invitations to ladies' meetings sponsored by Beth El, they perceived the Reform women as cliquish and described themselves as socially "freezing to death." By 1916, the eastern Europeans felt themselves well enough established to organize a congregation of their own, Agudas Achim. The congregation held services at first in members' homes, then in various commercial buildings, especially above Rosenberg's Department Store. Many years passed, however, before the congregation was able to erect its own synagogue.

In one case, at least, Alexandria witnessed a scene that took place all too often in northern cities. Often a man would come over to America first, find a job, and then bring over his family as quickly as he could. In some instances, if the man were unmarried, the family would include parents, brothers, and sisters, and depending on how successful he had been, aunts, uncles, and cousins as well. If married, then his first obligation would be to bring over his wife and children. Sometimes things did not go according to this plan. The man may have had an arranged marriage in the Old Country, and in the freedom of America he met and fell in love with another woman. Sometimes he even married her and ignored his wife back in Russia. Sometimes the man, who had learned a little English and had bought "Amerikaner" clothes, worried that his wife would look like a greenhorn and was embarrassed at the prospect of her joining him.

In 1913 the *Alexandria Gazette* carried a front-page story entitled "Deserted Wife's Pathetic Story." A young woman, intending to join her husband in the United States, had immigrated with one of her children; two others had been left with her family in Russia. She managed to track the

Esther Scoll donned a black gown for her wedding about 1893. Black was the traditional color worn by Sephardic Jewish brides at that time. The first High Holidays services in the Newport News area had been held in the home of Louis Nachman, her husband-to-be, in 1890.

Peninsula Jewish Historical Society; gift of Donald Nachman and family

man she believed to be her husband to his grocery store in Alexandria, only to discover that he was living with another wife and their three children. When the man refused to recognize his Russian wife and suggested she was deranged, she, with guidance from Hebrew charities in New York and Washington, sought the arrest of her allegedly bigamist husband.

The arrival of Russians provided an economic boost to the Tidewater area as well. Beginning in 1883 one finds new businesses opening each year with the names of their Russian Jewish proprietors: B. M. Oser, Adolph Rosenbaum, Jacob Brenner, Charles Nachman, Max Levinson, Isaac Lipman, and others. In Newport News, Joseph Reyner quickly became a successful businessman and served as a member of the common council from 1910 to 1917; his son, Harry, was elected to the city council for seven consecutive terms starting in 1922 and in 1930 became the city's first Jewish mayor.

Solomon Nachman arrived in the United States in 1891 as a boy of sixteen. He started in the retail dry goods business as a clerk at $8 a month but with the aid of his brother opened a small retail store on Eighteenth Street in Newport News in 1893. He did well there and in 1914 built a large four-story department store on Washington Avenue at Thirtieth, which soon ranked third in the state in its volume of annual sales.

In one instance, the success of a Norfolk businessman directly benefited Richmond. In a striking example of just how well some Jews had been accepted into Virginia society, David Lowenberg had been named director general of the Jamestown Exposition of 1907, designed to mark the 300th anniversary of the English settling of North America. The principal owner of the Norfolk Hampton Roads Corporation that owned the exposition grounds (the same area that later formed the nucleus of the Norfolk Naval Base), Lowenberg worried about the availability of good hotel rooms to house the thousands of people expected to attend the exposition.

He had already taken over the Monticello Hotel in Norfolk and the hotel at Sewell's Point, but in the summer of 1904, as he and Emanuel Raab, a Richmond entrepreneur, sat on a verandah at a hotel in Atlantic City, they decided that Richmond would probably be where many of the visitors would want to stay. There were not enough good hotel rooms in Richmond, so Lowenberg promptly bought a $307,000 option on the Jefferson Hotel on Franklin Street, a once proud and elegant building fallen on lean times after a devastating fire in 1901. Lowenberg, Joseph Bryan, and Joseph Willard, the lieutenant governor of Virginia and the owner of the posh Willard's Hotel in Washington, then formed the Jefferson Realty Corporation, bought the property, and began an unheard-of $1.5 million restoration of the hotel. The restoration, which can still be seen in the modern Jefferson, immediately brought the hotel back to, as one contemporary writer put it, "its lofty place at the top of the Richmond social scene."

In nearby Berkeley, David Glasser (originally Glaser) lived out the archetypical story of the eastern European immigrant. Following the imposition of the harsh anti-Semitic laws of the early 1880s, Glasser left Ligum, a small town in Lithuania, in 1885 and made his way to Baltimore. There he sought work to gather the money needed to bring the rest of his family over. The Baltimore Bargain House provided him with a backpack and items to sell, and Glasser headed for the so-called Upper Tract in West Virginia. He apparently did well, for in 1889 he returned to Russia to gather his wife, children, and other family members to bring them to the United States.

On his return, he took his family to Berkeley, at that time not even a town, across the Elizabeth River from Norfolk. Although there had been no history of Orthodox Lithuanians in the Tidewater area in the earlier nineteenth century, three of his landsmen (people from the same area of the Old Country) from Ligum had recently moved to the Hampton Roads area. These may have been relatives, but the fact that they had come from the same part of Russia gave Glasser a feeling that he and his family would not be in altogether alien surroundings. (These cousins, if that is what they were, had changed their names to sound less foreign and had chosen as their American name Legum—the name of the village in the Pale whence they had come.)

Glasser opened a store on Liberty Street, and he and his family lived upstairs. His daughter Ida worked with her parents in the store so that her brother Robert could attend medical school. (Dr. R. D. Glasser later became chief of gynecological services at St. Vincent DePaul Hospital). Ida Glasser married Philip Caplan and worked with him at his family's store, Caplan's Pharmacy. Other daughters also married locally and worked with their husbands in their hardware and grocery stores.

David Glasser lived to see his dream come true—to live freely as a Jew, to prosper because of his and his family's hard work, to see his children married and settled—and all in a place that neither he nor any of his neighbors or friends had ever heard of in Ligum—Berkeley, Virginia.

FROM JOY TO SORROW

THE early decades of the twentieth century were good ones for the commonwealth and for its various Jewish communities. Prosperous times and a national sense of optimism during the Progressive period did much to erase the lingering bitterness of the Civil War and Reconstruction years. New Jewish immigrants came into the state, not in overwhelming numbers, but slowly and steadily, reinforcing and expanding existing communities. By the early 1930s, approximately 25,000 Jews lived in Virginia, about 8,000 in Richmond, nearly that many in Norfolk, and the balance in smaller communities.

Looking back, we can see that the seeds of great turmoil later in the century were sown at this time, as Virginia and other southern states institutionalized Jim Crow laws, systematically separated black citizens, and reduced them to a second-class status. Although a few whites, Jew and Christian alike, may have been upset at this development, for the most part the white community accepted it as normal, just as two generations earlier it had accepted slavery.

What Virginia Jews could not have known in these halcyon days was that events across the ocean would soon affect them in ways neither they nor anyone else could have imagined.

One of the charming aspects of Virginia history is how slowly things change. There is a sense of history, a belief that although change may be good, there is no need to rush forward. Thus one finds that as late as the first decades of the twentieth century, peddlers still traveled through the small towns in the hills and valleys of the state, selling household goods from backpacks or wagons, much as earlier generations had done. On the eve of the First World War, Louis Zuckerman could still buy furs from farmers in the areas around Waynesboro and Winchester and sell pots, pans, and cloth to their wives.

The main area of Jewish economic growth continued to be in merchandising. The eastern European Jews opened stores in Alexandria, Newport News, Norfolk, Richmond, and smaller towns as well. In Charlottesville, according to one old-timer, "on Rosh Hashanah and Yom Kippur, you couldn't go outside because all the stores were closed. Everybody would

האשה רבקה בת ר' שמואל ז"ל,
הלכה לעולמה כ"ה ימים לחדש
טבת בשנו: תרע"ב
JANUARY 15 ℡, 1912.
NEWPORT NEWS VA.

Courtesy of Rita Spirn

This elaborate death certificate commemorates the passing of Rebecca Frank Mirmelstein (b. 1858) on 15 January 1912. She was the wife of Abraham Benson Mirmelstein, who became rabbi of Adath Jeshurun in Newport News in 1893.

close. . . . [T]here ain't nothing but Jewish stores back then." The Leterman Company, which by 1906 had a building containing 50,000 square feet of floor space, continued to dominate the city's commerce, but nearby one could find newer stores on Main Street—Walters's, Shapero's, Levy's, and others—as well as the still prosperous firms of Oberdorfer's and Kaufman's.

In the Tidewater area, Jewish businesses proliferated, and a listing of the stores that opened in Newport News between 1900 and the First World War would include Leon's Fine Clothing, the Morewitz Drug Store, Shapiro's Department Store, Kenneth Arch Real Estate, Sam Mirmelstein Clothier, the Family Shoe Store, and Brenner's Bakery. The community had become so prosperous that it built a new temple for Adath Jeshurun, which was formally dedicated on 19 September 1900, with Rabbi Edward N. Calisch of Richmond's Beth Ahabah conveying the blessings of the state's oldest congregation.

In many enterprises, the second and even the third generation began to take over the family business. In Richmond two of William Thalhimer's sons, Isaac and Moses, had grown up helping their father in the store.

Samuel Binswanger
Founder

Our confidence that "There Is A Bright Future For You And For Us" is firmly founded on the solid bed-rock of an ideal. An ideal forged by time, tested through the decades, surviving the ravages of seven of years- - -and now inexorably pressing forward and upward to greater heights.

Seventy-Five years ago, this ideal was born in the heart of our founder, Samuel Binswanger. It was based on his staunch faith in his fellow-Southerners, on his firm belief in the ultimate destiny of our own Southland, and on his unwavering confidence that he could prosper only by helping others to prosper through better serving their purpose.

Unfolded throughout the following pages, is the story of this ideal...its birth; its steady progress forward throughout chaotic years of panic, depressions, global upheavals; its fruition in the wide-spread success of today; and its bright promise of happy years lying ahead for you and for us.

To you of the South and Southwest who have made possible this outstanding record, and who have prospered along with us, we dedicate this saga of our Southland...And on this our Seventy-Fifth Anniversary we re-dedicate ourselves to a continuance of these high ideals of better serving your purpose.

Binswanger and Company

Beth Ahabah Museum and Archives

Binswanger and Company celebrated its seventy-fifth anniversary in 1947. Samuel Binswanger, Jr., a grandson of the founder, oversaw the transformation of a small retail store into a commercial empire employing more than a thousand people in several states.

Although they initially were partners in the enterprise, Isaac eventually bought his brother out and became the sole owner. In the late nineteenth century, Thalhimer's pioneered in the marketing of mass-produced, ready-to-wear clothing. Isaac began making regular trips to New York and offering his customers a wide range of ready-to-wear garments reflecting the latest fashions.

By 1917, Isaac Thalhimer presided over a good-sized emporium with a number of employees, and he brought his son William into the operation. A few years later father and son incorporated the business, and then in the 1920s the younger Thalhimer, along with Irving May, whom William had invited to join the company, began to transform what had essentially been a dry goods store into a modern department store with specialized departments to cater to specific customer preferences.

At Binswanger, the business founded by Samuel in 1872 passed into the control of his grandson and namesake. The younger Samuel had been afflicted with polio as a two-year-old, but he overcame that disability to oversee the enormous growth of the company. What had begun as a small retail store became, under his direction, a commercial empire with more than one thousand employees running operations in several states for the largest southern distributor of Libby-Owens-Ford glass products. Like so many others of that generation, Samuel Binswanger, Jr., took seriously his obligations both to the Jewish community and to the larger society; by the time of his death, he had been honored numerous times for his public works.

As Thalhimer's grew, so did other stores in the state capital. Beth Ahabah conducted a census of Jewish businesses in Richmond in 1909 that listed 287 retail and 15 wholesale merchants, 25 manufacturers, and 111 tailors. In 1900 the Chamber of Commerce elected Lewis Z. Morris as president; he headed the Savings Bank of Richmond, which was eventually absorbed by First and Merchants, the predecessor to NationsBank. By 1920, Jews could be found on the boards of directors of seven of the city's banks; William H. Schwarzschild headed the Central National Bank. Arthur J. Morris of Norfolk created the Morris Plan Bank, which became the Richmond-based Bank of Virginia (later absorbed by Signet). Richmond not only manufactured cigarettes but also in the early years of the century was home to the Kline Kar Corporation, which assembled family sedans until 1923.

The prominence of Jews in the commercial life of the state had its counterpart in public life. Jews served as members of the state assembly, on county and municipal councils and boards, and as appointed officials. During the Progressive era, when the indomitable Adèle Clark and Lila Meade Valentine led the struggle for woman's suffrage, Naomi Cohn, an early and enthusiastic fighter for women's rights, and other Jewish women marched at their side. Lawmaking was Cohn's passion for sixty years. Well after women secured the right to vote, she continued her work to improve working conditions for women and to abolish child labor. In 1993 the Virginia Business and Professional Women's Foundation named Cohn one of the first thirty honorees for the Women of Virginia Historic Trail.

The passage of the Nineteenth Amendment gave women new opportunities, and some rushed to seize them. Rebecca Pearl Lovenstein, for example, was one of the first two women to pass the bar examination in Virginia in 1920. In January 1925, she became the first woman to argue a case before the Virginia Supreme Court.

Growing anti-Semitism in the North, in the form of excluding Jews from certain clubs, hotels, and colleges, had its counterpart in the South as well, and one can find evidence of prejudice and exclusion in the commonwealth. Although Sol and Mortimer Kaufman were among the early members of the Farmington Club in Charlottesville, as the club became more exclusive, it restricted Jewish membership. The Kaufman brothers resigned in protest when a Jewish friend was blackballed. The Cavalier Club, the Princess Anne, and other bastions of Virginia society all closed their doors to Jews. The existence of a black underclass deflected some of the bias so prevalent

Naomi Cohn (1889–1982) was a tireless advocate of social reform. In 1923 she founded the Virginia Women's Council on State Legislation with fellow suffragist Adèle Clark.

Courtesy of Nancy Meyers Marsiglia

Foster Studio Collection, Virginia Historical Society

Rabbi Edward N. Calisch of Beth Ahabah addressed the Equal Suffrage League of Virginia at a rally on the steps of the state capitol in May 1915.

in the North, and some places, even while practicing exclusion, found room for some favored older customers.

For example, in the 1930s Samuel Wurtzel, the founder of Circuit City, was in business in the North. He often traveled to Virginia, where he had family, and liked to vacation at the Homestead, the exclusive resort in Hot Springs. At the time B'nai B'rith had accused it and other resorts of discriminating against Jews. Wurtzel stayed at the Homestead often and frequently played golf with the hotel's president, Tom Leonard. After one round, while the two men were changing their clothes in the locker room, Wurtzel asked Leonard about the hotel's policies, and Leonard told him that the resort did indeed discriminate, but not on the basis of religion. "We are particular about who we take," Leonard replied. "We like to take people who are recommended to us, not just anybody. But it isn't a question of religion, it's a question of the kind of people they are."

A short time later a young friend of Wurtzel, Robert Rosoff, and his wife went to Vermont on vacation and did not like it there. Rosoff, remembering that Wurtzel had suggested the Homestead, called the hotel's New York office to see if they had room and told the clerk that Wurtzel had recommended the resort. The clerk said he would check. A few minutes later the phone rang in Wurtzel's office, and one of the managers from the Homestead asked if he personally knew Rosoff and would recommend him to the hotel. Wurtzel said he did indeed know the young man and would be only too happy to endorse him. The hotel immediately called Rosoff to inform him that they had space, and the Rosoffs later reported to Wurtzel that they had had a wonderful time at the hotel and had been treated very well by both the management and the staff.

The fact that Sam Wurtzel and his friends could still stay at the Homestead did not mitigate the fact that that hotel and many other clubs and resorts in the Old Dominion adopted policies of keeping out Jews and in some instances Catholics as well. The state that had been at the forefront of ensuring religious freedom in the United States had apparently forgotten the lessons of Jefferson and Madison.

———

In 1914 the assassination of Archduke Franz Ferdinand of Austria-Hungary and his wife by a Serbian nationalist at Sarajevo plunged Europe into a war more horrible than any recorded to that time in mankind's history. Although initially all Americans wanted the United States to remain neutral, many Americans in the North of German descent, including the leading German Jewish families, quietly favored the Central Powers. Moreover, because Russia, the most autocratic country in Europe, fought on the side of the Allies, many Jews who had recently fled from

Ohef Sholom Temple, Norfolk

The Chamberlin Hotel in Hampton was among many Virginia establishments that barred Jews well into the twentieth century.

tsarist persecution also cheered on the Germans, as did many Christian immigrants from central Europe. A similar sentiment did not exist in the South, where the German Jews who had migrated in the nineteenth century had not kept up ties with the Fatherland. The *yahudim* in New York and Philadelphia had continued to speak German in their homes, maintain German-language schools for their children, and demand that their rabbis deliver sermons in the old tongue long after the German Jews of Virginia had given up these practices. When Woodrow Wilson asked Congress for a declaration of war in April 1917, Virginians flocked to the colors.

At home the Jewish communities rallied to support the war effort. The comments of Charles Hutzler in 1918 reflected that of leaders in Norfolk, Alexandria, the Valley, and other sites in the commonwealth:

> We have sent our boys to the front, we have sent them down to the seas, we have sent them aloft in the air. . . . We have made our donations to the Red Cross, to the Jewish Welfare Board, to the Y.M.C.A., we have aided to sustain the credit of the government by buying its bonds, we have done our share in conserving its resources, and have enlisted in the ranks of every organization which has given its willing service in behalf of humanity.

In 1941, when Beth Ahabah published *The Light Burns On* to mark both its centennial and the golden jubilee of Edward Calisch as its rabbi, it provided a list of what its members had done during the Great War. More than eighty men saw active service in the various branches of the armed services, while on the civilian front men and women directed local war bond drives, ran a warehouse for fruit stones used in the manufacture of gas

Volunteers provided critical relief during World War I. Eloise VanOs of Norfolk worked in the American Red Cross.

Ohef Sholom Temple, Norfolk

masks, arranged entertainments for troops at nearby army camps, served in local branches of the Council of National Defense, and donated their time and money to a variety of war-related activities. This list could easily have been duplicated by every congregation in the state.

The war also provided some of the more recent immigrants with a tangible method to display their allegiance to their new homeland. The *Alexandria Gazette* ran a number of articles and editorials extolling "Jewish Patriotism" as evinced by the number of local Jews enrolled in the military as well as by the local community's work in bond drives and other functions. One article quoted the mayor of a small town who explained why Jews and Christians were getting along so well: "It comes from reading the casualty lists," lists that included "all creeds and classes." The still small Alexandria community grieved greatly when it learned that the Lithuanian-born Max Fagelson had been gassed at Belleau Woods in 1918. Fagelson, fortunately, recovered and after the war opened a grocery store in Alexandria.

The Jews of Virginia also participated in special drives to help their brethren in the combat zones and in the Holy Land, although this latter campaign caused a great deal of tension within the communities, especially in those towns that had Reform congregations.

World War I challenged American Jewry in ways it could not have foreseen. All of the great Jewish populations of Europe were caught up in the war, and the battles, especially in the east, destroyed hundreds of towns

Ohef Sholom Temple, Norfolk

Congregation Ohef Sholom's temple on Monticello Avenue and Freemason Street in Norfolk, dedicated in 1902, was destroyed by fire on 12 February 1916.

and villages where Jews had lived for centuries. Although the western communities such as France, Germany, and England did not suffer comparable damage, the Jews of those countries were hard pressed to help out their own compatriots in need and had little left to give to help Jews in eastern and central Europe.

The United States, as a neutral country, could and did offer relief to both sides before American entry into the war in April 1917, and some charities were permitted to continue to provide aid in the war zones and in the east afterward as well. Led by the American Jewish Committee, an organization of the influential elite of the German Jewish community, American Jews raised millions of dollars for the war-ravaged communities of Europe through the American Jewish Relief Committee, which was later known as the Joint Distribution Committee. The war also led to the establishment of the National Jewish Welfare Board, which provided services to Jewish members of the military comparable to those provided by the YMCA.

Little controversy attended the raising of vast sums for the Jews of Europe. In the United States, those who had come over from Germany in the middle of the nineteenth century as well as those who had arrived more recently recognized ties of kinship with the suffering. As one speaker after another put it, "Had not we (or our parents) come to this blessed land, we too would now be suffering their fate." When it came to aiding the small Jewish colonies in Palestine, however, this unity fell apart.

The movement to reestablish a Jewish homeland in Palestine had begun in the 1880s and then had picked up momentum in the 1890s with the founding of the World Zionist Organization by Theodor Herzl. The Zionists sponsored the establishment of several small agricultural settlements in Palestine in the hope that they would grow and at some point in the future provide a nucleus around which an autonomous Jewish colony might form. These settlements had grown and by 1914 had established themselves economically as growers of citrus fruit and producers of wine, nearly all of which went to the European market, a market disrupted and cut off by the war.

The leaders of the relief effort did not oppose helping Jews in need, but they balked at helping the Palestinian colonies because of its implications. Many of the German-American leaders belonged to the Reform movement, and in 1885 the leaders of American Reform had met in Pittsburgh and adopted an eight-point platform, of which the fifth point not only rejected the traditional view of the Jewish people in exile but also denied any desire to return to Palestine: "We consider ourselves no longer a nation, but a religious community, and therefore expect neither a return to Palestine, nor a sacrificial worship under the sons of Aaron, nor the restoration of any of the laws concerning the Jewish state."

The Zionists, with their plan to reestablish a Jewish state, seemed to threaten the allegiance American Jews owed to the United States, and the leaders of the Reform movement as well as of the American Jewish Committee feared that their status as American citizens might be compromised by so-called dual allegiance. This issue remained a concern in the American Jewish community from the beginning of the century until after the establishment of the State of Israel in 1948.

The fears of Reform Jews had been heightened during the war by several developments. First, there had been the rise of a strong American Zionist movement under the leadership of Boston reformer Louis D. Brandeis, whom President Wilson named to the Supreme Court in 1916. Brandeis had developed a uniquely American view of Zionism that called on the Jews of the United States to be loyal to their new homeland and supportive of the efforts to build a new and democratic society in Palestine. By undercutting the fear of dual allegiance, Brandeis apparently negated one of the major objections of the German Jewish community to Zionism.

Ohef Sholom Temple, Norfolk

Peninsula Jewish Historical Society

Above: In 1916 Ohef Sholom in Norfolk formed Boy Scout Troop No. 11, shown here about 1920.

Left: Rodef Sholom Temple Sisterhood organized a Girl Scout troop in the early 1930s. The troop from Newport News is shown here about 1951.

Second, the members of the Zionist Organization of America came primarily from the eastern European immigrants, and this factor further worried the *yahudim*, who saw this as another aspect of the "un-American" nature of Zionism. Most worrisome to them, however, was the success of American and European Zionist leaders during the war in convincing the British government, which conquered Palestine, to announce in the Balfour Declaration of November 1917 that it favored the establishment of a Jewish homeland in Palestine after the war.

The Reform response was immediate and antagonistic. At the 1918 meeting of the Central Conference of American Rabbis, the umbrella group of Reform rabbis, the membership adopted a resolution that declared in part that "we do not subscribe to the phrase in the declaration which says 'Palestine is to be a national home land for the Jewish people.' We hold that Jewish people are and of right ought to be at home in all lands." The chair of the committee presenting this resolution, Edward N. Calisch of Richmond, was a bitter foe of Zionism all his life, and he made Beth Ahabah into a fortress against Zionist ideas. Well after the establishment of the State of Israel, the congregation had a reputation of not supporting the new Jewish state.

In other Reform congregations a similar spirit prevailed. In Norfolk, where Louis Mendoza served as rabbi of Ohef Sholom from 1907 to 1945, a mass meeting of all the Jewish congregations was convened shortly after the end of the war to raise money for the ravaged European communities. Eva Leon, a member of the American Zionist movement, had recently returned from investigating conditions in the Holy Land, and she asked permission to speak on behalf of the settlements. At first the sponsors balked and declared that the bylaws of Ohef Sholom forbade the occupation of the pulpit by a lay person. After it was pointed out that other lay people would be speaking from the pulpit, the committee grudgingly allowed her to speak but warned her not to exceed thirty minutes and not to say anything that might offend the Christian community. An effective orator, Leon saw her efforts rewarded by the organization of a committee in the Tidewater area to collect money for Palestine.

———

The Twenties saw a period of marked prosperity for the commonwealth, and the Jewish communities and businessmen around the state found the decade a good one for individual as well as communal growth. New stores went up, such as the Kaufman specialty store on Broad Street in Richmond, while older businesses, such as the Binswanger Glass Company, expanded into other states.

Charles M. Guggenheimer's store in Lynchburg opened in 1881 in the first iron-front building erected in the city.

Virginia Historical Society

Many new businesses also started during this decade, some of which failed in the Depression while others continued to grow. Samuel Markel saw a great opportunity in the enormous expansion of automobile and truck traffic. Many veterans without jobs had bought used cars and hired themselves out as drivers of jitneys, passenger cars that ran regular routes. In Norfolk, as in Richmond, the city trolley lines naturally opposed this new competition and managed to get the city council to curtail jitneys by requiring them, among other things, to carry public liability insurance.

Markel decided to organize the Norfolk jitney operators. After he talked on street corners and to many of them individually, the drivers held a mass meeting at which they elected him their president. He drew up a code for motor-vehicle regulations that the city council adopted, but it did not repeal the insurance requirement. No underwriters, however, wanted to issue such insurance, because, as one person put it, "the insuring of jitneys at that time was as hazardous as leading a bull through a china shop."

To remedy the situation, Markel founded an insurance company, the Mutual Casualty Association, but had trouble getting financing in Norfolk. Finally a Richmond bank offered him $50,000 on two conditions: first, the jitney operators had to sign the notes, and second, Markel had to retire the loan at the rate of $1,000 a week. Every Monday morning he rushed out to collect the $5 premiums from the operators and shoved the pile of small bills through the bank teller's cage before closing.

Markel had been right, though, in his vision that the automobile would transform American society, and the Richmond-based American Fidelity and Casualty Company became one of the biggest underwriters of commercial vehicles in the country. Markel's four sons joined him in the business, which by 1952 had assets of $24 million and insured 62,000 trucks and buses throughout the United States and more than 100,000 drivers. In the nearly fifty years since, the Markel Agency has branched out into other forms of insurance underwriting.

In many places, congregations felt prosperous enough either to put up new synagogue buildings or to expand existing structures. In Staunton, for example, Abraham Weinberg announced after services one day in 1924, "I'm tired of worshiping in something that looks like a warehouse. I'll put up half the money for a real temple if the congregation will put up the other half." He did; they did; and the Jews of Temple House of Israel soon had a new building, one they are still using today.

In Alexandria, the Russian Jewish community prospered, but as it did so, internal bickering also increased. Some of the members of Agudas Achim formed a splinter group, Beth Israel, which in 1927 purchased a building on the southwest corner of Wolfe and South Pitt streets, which it could not afford. The following year the two groups reunited, and the reconstituted Agudas Achim took over control of the Wolfe Street property. It then launched a successful campaign to renovate the antebellum structure and at the dedication ceremony recognized members of the larger community who had contributed nearly $700 to the drive.

The attractiveness of Virginia to European Jews did not cease after the imposition of the National Quotas Act of 1924, which cut off nearly all immigration from southern and eastern Europe and barred those already in the United States from bringing over additional family members. This restriction did not stop one woman, who made her way from Russia to Canada by passing herself off as the maid of another passenger on the ship. From there she had no difficulty entering the United States. A prearranged marriage to her cousin, who had immigrated a number of years earlier, allowed her to remain in Alexandria for the rest of her life. Even as an old woman, however, she still feared being identified as an illegal alien and being deported.

So long as they could, Jews from Europe migrated to the United States, and some of them found their way south. The older German community in Fredericksburg, for example, was itself invigorated by an influx of eastern Europeans following the war, as was Bristol, where the newcomers provided the support needed to build a synagogue for Temple B'nai Sholom.

The good times for Virginia and indeed for the country and the world came crashing to a halt in the fall of 1929. Historians now recognize that the prosperity of the Twenties had rested on shaky foundations and that eventually the combination of too much factory expansion, excessive margin purchases on the stock market, a weak agricultural economy, and maldistribution of income would have led to collapse. But no one, even those who had been concerned about a runaway economy, could have imagined the extent of the Depression that followed.

The Jews in Virginia again have no domestic history during the Great Depression that is different from that of their Christian neighbors. Those

Abe Horowitz (1866–1936) came to Newport News in 1896 and entered the mercantile business. He founded the Newport News Base Ball Club primarily to entertain immigrants coming to work at the Newport News Shipbuilding and Dry Dock Company.

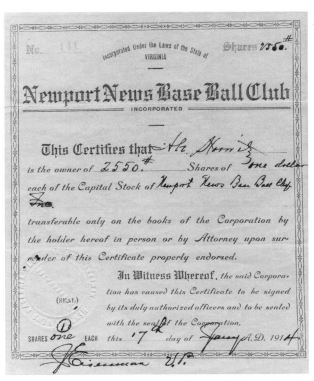

Peninsula Jewish Historical Society

Solomon Nachman (1874–1929) founded a department store in Newport News in 1893 and brought his wife, Ida (1879–1954), into the business after they were married in 1898. In 1929 he began an expansion of his business but died before the new store was completed. His wife took over management of Nachman's, and a bronze tablet placed in the new store honored its founder.

Virginia Historical Society

businesses that had resisted overexpansion and kept tight control of their costs weathered the storm; those that did not, as well as many small shops where the owners had no backup resources, went under. In the spring of 1929 Solomon Nachman designed and began construction of a new building at the corner of Thirty-second Street and Washington Avenue in Newport News so he could expand his prosperous business. In May he died suddenly, and his wife, Ida Solomon Nachman, took over as president of the store and carried out her late husband's wishes. She oversaw the completion of the building in the heart of the Depression and kept the business afloat throughout the lean years.

Most congregations also had to cut back on their work. The older established congregations, such as Beth Ahabah in Richmond and Ohef Sholom in Norfolk, weathered the troubles; others did not do as well. In Lynchburg, for example, at the beginning of 1929 Agudath Sholom approved a budget for the coming year of $6,500, which included $3,000 for

Peninsula Jewish Historical Society; gift of Bernice Evenson

The cast of the first Rodef Sholom cabaret, sponsored by Rodef Sholom Temple, included sons and daughters of many of the first Jewish families to settle in Newport News in the late nineteenth century. The master of ceremonies (center) was Harry Reyner, who served on the city council 1922–46 and was the first Jewish mayor of Newport News, 1930–32.

the salary of its rabbi, Dr. Irvin M. Melamed. Even before the stock market crashed, the congregation could not meet the budget, and Melamed could not afford to stay on with a reduced salary. His successor, Charles Abeles, also had to leave when the congregation could not pay him. As the Depression continued, it looked for a while as if the congregation would lose its synagogue, because it did not have the funds to meet its mortgage payments. Fortunately, the bank proved willing to renegotiate the mortgage, and Agudath Sholom managed to make its way through the hard times. At the same time, the members also raised enough money so that the congregation could once again hire a full-time rabbi.

Virginia Jews, however, did have one additional worry that did not, at least immediately, affect others—Adolf Hitler and the Nazi party in Germany. The story of the rise of fascism in Europe is well known, as is Hitler's monomaniacal obsession with Jews and Judaism, an obsession that led to a series of anti-Semitic laws and riots that culminated in the extermination of six million European Jews. At the start, few people—Jew or gentile—took the Nazis seriously. Even after the National Socialists came to power in 1933, most Germans did not believe Hitler would attempt to carry out his more extravagant campaign promises. Rather, they believed that once in power he would temporize and find that the exigencies of ruling Germany precluded his pursuing dreams of world power or of making Germany and Europe *Judenrein*. In 1935, however, a series of racial restrictions, known as the Nuremberg Laws, excluded Jews from universities, government jobs, and many other sectors of the economy and reduced them to a second-class status. Although resistance to the Nazis' initial outbursts of anti-Semitism caused Hitler to back off, following the 1936 Olympics, when Germany put on its best face to the world, the Führer felt confident enough to pursue his dreams.

By 1938, the military might of the Third Reich had grown to the point that Hitler forced the western powers to back down in face of his demands for the Czech Sudetenland. The following year he attacked Poland and plunged the world into six years of global warfare. In 1941, at a secret meeting in Wannsee, the Reich embarked on the Final Solution, designed to kill off every Jewish man, woman, and child in Germany and in the territories conquered by the Wehrmacht. Although news about the mass killings began seeping out of Europe even during the war, the full extant of the Nazi horror did not become known until 1945, when Allied troops liberated the concentration camps, and newspapers and magazines brought the story to an amazed and horrified world.

Some German Jews believed that Hitler would never act against them. After all, they and their families had lived in Germany for hundreds of years, they had fought for the Fatherland in 1870 and in 1914, they had contributed to the culture and prosperity of what they considered their country. For many of these people, the realization that Hitler meant what he said came too late, and they perished in the camps. For others, mostly younger Germans, fear of the Nazis led them to leave, but with a world wracked by economic depression, where would they go? The Jewish colonies in Palestine wanted them, but the British, trying to appease the Arabs, would not let in more than a few thousand. The United States, as a result of the quota sections of the 1924 immigration law, looked on Germany more favorably than on eastern Europe, but the numbers who could enter the country legally were far below the demand for visas.

One lucky young man was Eric Lipman, who later joked that he was the only refugee to come to the United States with a full set of dinner clothes, a wardrobe of hand-tailored suits, and six Leica cameras. German law did not allow Jewish émigrés to take more than a few dollars in cash but did permit them to take as many of their possessions as they could carry. Lipman's family, which owned a factory in rural Germany, managed to get him a visa and then bought him clothes so that he would not look like a beggar in America. The Leicas, then considered the best camera in the world, could be sold for cash once he got here. Lipman was one of the lucky ones, and he repaid his new country by joining the army and serving in the

Flora Frenkel and her family fled Nuremberg about 1938. After arriving in Newport News, she registered as an alien.

intelligence section. In 1945 he was one of the first American soldiers to enter the concentration camp at Theresienstadt. After his discharge, he eventually settled in Richmond.

The Jews of Virginia as well as their brethren in other parts of the country did their best to help the suffering Jews of Germany and later of Poland and to bring at least some of them to the United States. But to do that required money and people willing to sign bonds guaranteeing that the new immigrants would have a job and not become a public charge. This work was done both communally and individually.

In Richmond, Jews managed to overcome the social and institutional fragmentation that had increasingly marked the community. German Jews, affiliated primarily with Beth Ahabah, considered themselves as patrons of the newcomers, despite the fact that some of the newcomers had been in the commonwealth for five decades and had American-born children and even grandchildren. The Ladies Hebrew Benevolent Association of Beth Ahabah, the oldest charitable organization in Virginia, handled several hundred cases every year. The National Council of Jewish Women operated Neighborhood House, a settlement house founded in 1912 to serve the children of eastern European immigrants. In addition, other charitable groups, either freestanding or associated with one of the Orthodox synagogues or the recently established Conservative congregation Beth-El, served particular clienteles in the community. There was no coordination of services, and in the midst of the Depression, many of these groups found the demand exceeding their resources. They had to come up with additional help in an effort to rescue at least some European Jews.

As early as 1938, long before many others in the United States recognized what was happening, Edward N. Calisch, then in his fifth decade as rabbi of Beth Ahabah, warned not only his fellow Jews but also the wider community of the tragedy then unfolding in Europe. He chose to deliver this message in a brotherhood address at the First Baptist Church. "It is the conscience of America," Calisch declared,

> that will not permit to go unrebuked conduct that shames humanity itself, that will not be silent when the very principles of democracy are challenged by the madness of totalitarian governments. It is the conscience of America that protests in no uncertain tones against the brutal persecutions of defenseless minorities, against the savage butchery of the concentration camps, the relentless expropriation of every means of livelihood, the searing of the souls of little children by heartless humiliation.

Following the talk, the congregation of First Baptist joined in a collection for the benefit of the Joint Distribution Committee.

By then, however, the Richmond Jewish Community Council, the predecessor of the current Jewish Community Federation, had been formed to coordinate fund-raising and charitable work within the community. It is difficult to tell whether the impetus for organization came from within the community or at the suggestion of the National Council of Jewish Federations and Welfare Funds, which was then attempting to coordinate fund-raising and help for European Jews on a national basis. Whatever the reason, the city's Jewish organizations, although jealously retaining their autonomy, recognized that in this crisis they had to act together. It would be a lesson well learned and invaluable after the war. The short-term results also proved instructive. Within three years the council announced an annual fund-raising goal of $50,000—a large sum during the Depression— and exceeded the quota by $13,000.

An editorial that appeared in the *Richmond News Leader* provides insight on how the leaders of the city felt about the Jewish community. Under the heading "The Jewish Fund," the editors wrote:

> A devoted member of the Richmond Jewish Community called the other day at The News Leader to explain this week's campaign for funds to aid Jewish philanthropies in the United States and abroad. 'We shall not,' said he, 'burden the paper with the details of the campaign, because our appeal is to a small element of readers.' We told him as strongly as we could that he was mistaken. A cause that concerns so many million human beings at the darkest period in their modern history is certain to elicit the full sympathy of all Richmonders. In every general campaign in Richmond—whether for the Community Fund, the Shelter-

ing Arms, the Crippled Children's Hospital or any of the institutions of higher learning—citizens of Jewish faith have been alive to their obligations. Never have they failed to cooperate. If now, in their modesty, they limit their solicitation to their co-religionists, they are not limiting interest in the same measure. They may be sure when they meet this evening in the Jefferson Auditorium . . . that all Richmond will be there in spirit—to approve and encourage.

The editorial apparently had an effect, because at the end of the campaign the directors of the council publicly acknowledged that some of the money had come from outside the community, and they wanted to thank their Christian neighbors for "this gesture of friendship and fellowship."

Giving money to the council was all that some people could afford, but for others who had the resources and the determination, more had to be done. The chief goal of many individuals and committees in these years was to bring Jews from Europe and to save them from Nazi atrocities. Between 1934 and 1943, Virginia took in between four and five hundred refugees who had managed to escape. Some 328 of them settled in Richmond. (About two-thirds of them remained in the city permanently; the rest resettled elsewhere in the United States after the war, returned to Europe, or moved to Israel.) A national coordinating committee, under the overall direction of the Hebrew Immigrant Aid Society, supervised the rescue operation, while committees in local communities took care of finding places for the newcomers to live and to work. Individual Jewish businessmen signed affidavits guaranteeing financial support for the refugees, an obligation that at least in the mid-Thirties put a great strain on some of them.

In Roanoke, Arthur Taubman, who ran three auto parts stores, helped several hundred Jews escape from Europe by swearing to immigration authorities that they were all his cousins. In Staunton, the formidable doyenne of the community, Fannie Strauss, quietly raised money for the passage of German refugees to America, helped settle them in the Valley, and then subsidized them until they could earn their own way.

In 1936 William Thalhimer, who was national co-chairman of the Resettlement Division of the National Coordinating Committee for Refugees, set out to do something more specific and with his cousin, Morton G. Thalhimer, Sr., bought Hyde Park Farm, a 1,500-acre farm near Burkeville. With help from Congressman David E. Satterfield, Jr., of Richmond, Supreme Court Justice Felix Frankfurter, and others, Thalhimer undertook the arduous task of getting at least some younger Jews out of Germany and to the United States.

He contacted Curt Bondy, head of a Jewish agricultural school in Gross Breesen, Germany, which taught youngsters farming to prepare them for life in Palestine or some other country to which they could escape. Just as Hitler began to step up his anti-Jewish program, however, Brazil and other

Temple Beth-El, Richmond

Choir Director Morris Bandas conducted the music at Beth-El's first Rosh Hashanah service in Columbo Hall in 1931. Cantor Solomon Shapiro stands on the left and Rabbi Joseph Raffaeli on the right.

countries closed their doors to further immigration; then the Nazis seized the school in Gross Breesen and turned it into a forced labor camp. The only hope for the would-be farmers was the Virginia plan, as it was known in Germany.

Thalhimer somehow managed to obtain visas and arrange for forty young Jews to leave Germany and to come to Hyde Park Farm. He signed the guarantee papers and to make the children welcome even sent his wife's piano to the farm for them to play. The lucky ones who made it to Hyde Park Farm remained there for varying periods of time, some for a few weeks and others for about four years. Soon after the United States declared war on Germany in December 1941, nearly all of the young men enlisted in the army to fight Hitler, while the women took defense jobs in the cities.

In March 1990 several of the original Hyde Park refugees returned for their first reunion in half a century. One alumnus, George Landeker, summed up the feelings of all of them: "Thalhimer saved many of us from death. There is simply no other way to say it."

Regrettably, this generous act caused some local anti-Semites to spread rumors that Thalhimer had fired his native-born workers in order to hire immigrants. To quash the story as quickly as possible, Thalhimer called a meeting of all his employees. He assured them that not one of the immigrants at the farm would be working at the store and that even if he wanted to fire his current employees, he was "too good of a businessman to do it."

The anti-Semitism involved in this event was of a different order from the social prejudice that had led to the closing of some clubs to Jews. This policy had, unfortunately, become all too common in many parts of the United States in the 1930s, although when the Chamberlin resort in Old Point Comfort barred Jews, Senator Harry F. Byrd, Sr., attacked the practice. But in Virginia and elsewhere in the 1930s, fascist groups inspired by the success of the Nazis sprang up and called on Americans to adopt racial policies against the Jews similar to those espoused by the Third Reich. In Virginia the periodical *Southern Progress*, edited by Richmond attorney I. Sheppard Potts, trumpeted a pro-Nazi, anti-Semitic line. "The secret of German success," the magazine maintained, "is that the German people have freed themselves from Jewish control. . . . The entire world may do likewise." Despite the existence of such hate mongers, in 1940 a representative of the American Jewish Committee wrote that "Richmond, like most Southern Communities, has been extraordinarily free of the sort of [anti-Semitic] agitation with which Northern and Eastern cities have become all too familiar in the last couple of years."

Because rabbis were at even greater risk in Nazi Germany than other Jews, the national Jewish religious organizations made a special effort to bring them out. Alexandria's Congregation Beth El was able to help one such rabbi and in return secured itself a spiritual leader for a number of years.

The synagogue had been without a rabbi of its own for many years and had relied on lay leaders or student rabbis from Hebrew Union College. In an effort coordinated by the Reform movement, American congregations took on German rabbis either as assistants or as full-time clerics. Hugo Schiff had been born near Heidelberg, received a doctorate in theology from the university there, and later earned a doctorate in philosophy from the Frederick Alexander University for a treatise on Ralph Waldo Emerson. He then served for a number of years as rabbi in Karlsruhe, the capital of Baden. A week after *Kristallnacht*, the night of broken glass on 10 November 1938, when Nazi-inspired mobs ransacked and burned Jewish synagogues and businesses, Irving Diener, the secretary of Beth El, wrote to Schiff to inform him that the congregation would like to hire him as rabbi at a salary of $1,800 a year. He also enclosed the necessary documentation so that Schiff could get a visa to the United States.

The undertaking was a daring, some might even say foolhardy, venture for a congregation that at the time had only twenty-three members. A special solicitation, over and above the annual dues of $36, brought in $670. The Hebrew Benevolent Society gave some more, and there was also a

A week after *Kristallnacht*, the night of broken glass on 10 November 1938, Beth El in Alexandria offered Dr. Hugo Schiff, a rabbi in Karlsruhe, the capital of Baden, the post of spiritual leader of their congregation. Schiff served Beth El for nearly a decade before moving to the Washington Hebrew Congregation.

Beth El Hebrew Congregation Archives, Alexandria

generous response from the gentile community. Declaring that the members of Beth El "have honored yourself, won the admiration of your city, and made closer the fellowship of God's people herein," the Reverend John P. Tyler, minister of Alexandria's Washington Street Methodist Church, asked the privilege, both personally and on behalf of his congregation, of sharing the support of the new rabbi.

It took several months before all of the arrangements could be made, but eventually Schiff and his wife arrived in Alexandria, and he took up his duties as rabbi. He also brought with him a Torah he had saved from the destruction of his synagogue in Karlsruhe during *Kristallnacht*. Schiff served Beth El for nearly a decade before moving to the Washington Hebrew Congregation.

Another Virginia congregation also secured the services of a survivor, but somewhat later. When the 82d Airborne Division liberated the concentration camp at Wobbelin, they found a young teenager, Laslo Berkowits, and their care helped him to survive. Berkowits later immigrated to the United States, and after serving in the United States Army, he attended the University of Cincinnati and Hebrew Union College. Following his ordination in 1963, he joined a new Reform congregation in northern Virginia, Rodef Shalom in Falls Church, and has been there ever since. Today when he talks about the Holocaust and people ask, "Where was God at Auschwitz?" Berkowits says that God was there. The more important question is, "Where was Man?"

Not just Jews reached out to help the victims of Nazism. Hans Schmitt had been born in 1921 to a well-to-do family. His father, a successful businessman, was a gentile, while his mother came from a Jewish family and was one of Germany's first female doctors of law. The Nazis hated such mixed marriages, and Schmitt's parents prudently sent him to Holland for his education. When the war broke out, he managed to get to America. Once in this country he decided not to live in New York and began casting about for a college to attend. One day he opened the mail to find a letter to a social worker friend of the family from Francis Pendleton Gaines, the president of Washington and Lee University, requesting that Schmitt enroll there. As Schmitt put it, "This sounded almost too good to be true. The administration of Washington and Lee, one of the oldest schools in the country, actually suggested that I might do them a favor by enrolling." The school sent an alumnus to visit him and convince him to attend. Schmitt departed for Lexington and in his memoirs recalls his arrival in Virginia at six o'clock in the morning:

> There was not a human being in sight. . . . I passed the president's house, on whose garage I discovered a plaque reminding the passerby that it had once been the stable of Robert E. Lee's horse Traveler. I was amazed. Where I came from, the habitats of emperors, statesmen and other national heroes often bore such memorial reminders ... but the stall of a defeated general's horse had never figured among the revered places I had visited in my childhood. I was perplexed, and wondered what uncommon virtues had entitled this humble beast to such distinction.

Eventually Schmitt learned about Traveler and also learned how warm and hospitable a small Virginia community could be to a refugee youngster.

In 1940 the good people of the Tidewater, and through them the entire country, learned of the fear that fleeing refugees had of life under Nazi rule. On 9 August of that year, a Portuguese passenger ship, the SS *Quanza*, left Lisbon with 317 refugees, including a number of prominent artists, civic leaders, and intellectuals. When the ship docked in New York on 19 August, 196 passengers, the lucky owners of American visas, disembarked.

Peninsula Jewish Historical Society

Rose Schamroth and her daughters, Malvina and Annette, gazing through the porthole of the Portuguese vessel *Quanza*, were among eighty refugees from Nazi persecution whose vessel was turned away in Mexico and initially at Norfolk. Newport News maritime attorney Jacob L. Morewitz got them temporary visas to enter the United States. Most were able to stay permanently, but to prevent repetition of the incident, the national government adopted policies that effectively closed the United States to Jews trying to flee Nazi persecution. Malvina Schamroth Parnes and Annette Schamroth Lachman, shown as adults on the right, now live in New York.

The remaining refugees had transit papers to Veracruz, but when the *Quanza* reached the Mexican port later in the month, President Lázaro Cárdenas del Rio refused to allow all but a few refugees to land, despite the efforts of American ambassador Josephus Daniels and Stephen S. Wise, president of the American Jewish Congress.

Wise then turned to the American government and asked Secretary of State Cordell Hull to help. The secretary agreed to do what he could and to monitor the ship's movements. The *Quanza* in the meantime had left Veracruz and rather than going to Nicaragua, where American officials thought she was headed, actually was steaming toward Hampton Roads to take on coal for the journey back across the Atlantic. There the captain, Alberto Harberts, ordered the detention of all passengers and crew against their will. One passenger, Hillman Wolff, a German Jew, had anticipated such detention might happen and jumped overboard. After battling surf and current he reached Old Point, but a guard at Fort Monroe took him back to the boat. Soon afterward, local attorneys filed petitions for habeas corpus on behalf of four passengers.

A Newport News lawyer, Jacob L. Morewitz, who had an admiralty practice with his wife, Sallie, had been contacted by a New York attorney on behalf of Moritz Rand and his family. Morewitz entered a libel for $100,000 against the ship. He argued that the *Quanza* had breached its contract with the Rands because they had not been allowed to land in Veracruz. In subsequent hearings Morewitz also argued that Captain Harberts had violated the so-called *Roxen* doctrine that provided shore leave for foreign seamen while their ships docked in American ports. Morewitz later told his sons that he did not believe he could ultimately win the case on admiralty grounds but that he wanted to tie the ship up in dock long enough for Jewish groups to put pressure on Washington to let the *Quanza* passengers disembark in the United States. The strategy worked; when the judge set a $5,000 bond on the ship, it took several days for the owner's attorney to wire Lisbon for the money and to receive a response. Judge Luther B. Way, who presided over the case, later noted that had the libel suit not been filed, "that vessel would very probably have left this jurisdiction" with the refugees still on board.

Franklin Roosevelt, in the middle of his campaign for an unprecedented third term as president, initially wanted to ignore the *Quanza*, but with the ship tied up by an American court he could not do so. Moreover, his wife and conscience, Eleanor Roosevelt, interceded on the refugees' behalf. While the FBI warned about potential subversives on board and polls showed that the American people did not want the immigration quotas expanded, at the same time the daily newspapers carried heartrending stories about the plight of the people aboard. The Norfolk *Virginian-Pilot* ran a story titled "Family Separated by Stern Laws of U.S." and showed Rose Schamroth and her two daughters, Malvina and Annette, staring wistfully out through a porthole at their husband and father, who was trying to touch them.

To avoid further embarrassment, the administration ordered James G. McDonald, chairman of the President's Advisory Committee on Political Refugees, and a small committee to work out a plan to evaluate the immigrant status of the *Quanza* passengers and to allow all of the people on board the ship temporary landing permits. Because of the increased risk of transatlantic travel caused by the rise in German U-boat activity, the government eventually decided that none of the passengers would have to return to Europe.

Congregation Agudath Sholom, Lynchburg

The Sisterhood for Jewish Servicemen at Camp Pickett organized seders during World War II.

Thus, even before the full horror of the Holocaust had become known, Virginians had learned firsthand how the Nazis disrupted and terrorized the lives of innocent people who wanted nothing more than to live peacefully and freely. The Jews of the commonwealth, trying as best they could to save even a few of those threatened by the Nazis, must have thought often of how different their lives would have been had not they or their ancestors made the trip to the New World.

Once the United States entered the war in December 1941, Americans of all walks of life answered the call to arms, and there is not a single congregation in the state that did not send off several of its members to fight against the Axis. A number even lost their rabbis; Ohef Sholom's assistant rabbi, Joseph Levenson, resigned to become a chaplain.

On the home front the stories of the Second World War are similar to those of the First—shortages, making do, worrying about husbands and fathers and sons in the service, working in war plants, and trying to do all one could to make victory come a day sooner. Helping the war effort was mostly a serious business, but every now and then one could find a lighter side to the news.

The Norfolk area, with its enormous naval base, became a major port for the military, and the city was inundated not only with military personnel, but also with some less desirable entrepreneurs. One of the busiest places in the city was the red-light district on East Main Street, and the navy worried as it saw the venereal disease rate among sailors climb to 117 per thousand.

Dudley Cooper was then trying to build an amusement park at Ocean View. He suddenly discovered that the navy had a major interest in his success. The brass believed that if sailors had a healthy alternative to the red-light district, they would go there instead, and the health problems could be alleviated. The allures of Ocean View Amusement Park seemed to trump those of the downtown area, and the venereal rate dropped from 117 down to thirty-four cases per thousand by the end of 1943.

For the sailors who came to Ocean View, it was a pleasant interlude as they waited to ship out, and no doubt many of them, as they enjoyed the rides, wondered what life would be like after the war ended.

Courtesy of Rita Beskin Cogan

Virginia G. Hofheimer of Norfolk was a plane spotter during World War II.

YEARS OF TURMOIL

THE decades following the Allied triumph in World War II should have been good ones for the United States, for Virginia, and for the commonwealth's Jewish communities. In some ways they were, as the nation enjoyed nearly a quarter century of prosperity. Projects begun before the war, in some cases before the Depression, came to fruition. Men and women who had interrupted their lives to fight fascism picked up the threads, started families, opened businesses, bought houses, and enjoyed the unparalleled material success that marked American society from 1945 to about 1970.

For the nation as a whole, however, what should have been years of bliss were corroded by the Cold War, the threat of atomic conflict, and a small but real war in Korea, while on the domestic front Americans confronted first the McCarthy witch hunts and then the civil rights struggle. Southerners in particular felt the full effect of this last movement, which attempted to wipe away centuries of degradation and secure full equality for America's black citizens. In addition, American Jews had to come to terms with the Holocaust, the full details of which became known only after the liberation of the death camps, and then the struggle to establish the State of Israel and maintain its security. The creation of the Jewish state and the civil rights movement made the postwar decades years of turmoil for the Jews of Virginia.

As soldiers returned from the battlefields in 1945, they wanted to resume normal lives as quickly as possible. But the world they came home to differed in many ways from the one they had left in 1941 or 1942. One of the positive things they found was that as a result of several initiatives enacted by Congress, veterans of the Second World War would be well thanked by a grateful nation. One program that had a profound effect on Jews was the G.I. Bill of Rights. Although the older, more prosperous German Jewish community had been able to send its children to college for several generations, the children of the eastern European immigrants had not been as fortunate. Many had indeed gone to state-sponsored schools in the 1920s and 1930s, but the Depression had made it difficult for less well-off families to keep their sons and daughters in college. The G.I. Bill provided millions of men and women the opportunity they might never

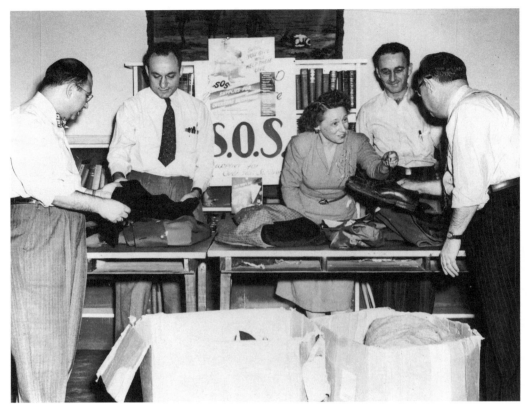

Peninsula Jewish Historical Society

In December 1947, volunteers in Newport News packed supplies for the relief of overseas survivors of the Holocaust.

have otherwise had to attend college or graduate school. Jews in particular rushed to take advantage of this chance, seeing it as one more piece of evidence of how America treated them as equal citizens. The country had called on them to serve, and it would thank them for having done so.

At the University of Virginia, long home to upper-class youths seemingly more intent on partying than on studying, the arrival of the veterans completely changed the nature of the student body for several years. These were serious young men who had risked their lives and who intended to take full advantage of the educational opportunities Mr. Jefferson's university provided. The university's Jewish population had been climbing steadily through the twentieth century and grew even more steeply after 1945. A Jewish Student Union had been established in 1939, and in 1941 it became one of the first collegiate chapters of the B'nai B'rith Hillel Foundation. The influx of Jewish students after 1945 led Hillel to expand and acquire its current facilities at the school.

Edward Elson, who graduated from the college in 1956 and later became the first Jewish rector of the university, recalled that the biggest obstacle facing Jewish students in the decade after the war was the dominant position fraternities enjoyed not only in the school's social life but also in controlling student politics and organizations. "If you were not in a fraternity, you were out," Elson said. "Jews were excluded from the

Holsinger Studio Collection (#9862), Special Collections Department, Manuscript Division,
University of Virginia Library

Zeta Beta Tau, the first Jewish fraternity at the University of Virginia, was established in 1915. Before the founding of chapters of ZBT and Phi Epsilon Pi, Jewish students were banned from existing fraternities.

fraternities and restricted to membership in three Jewish fraternities, so their political involvement was limited."

This exclusion may not have upset the veterans too much; they had more important things on their minds. But as the wave of G.I. Bill enrollees passed and the student body reverted to recent high school graduates, this discrimination rankled. The four Jewish fraternities—Alpha Epsilon Pi, Zeta Beta Tau, Phi Epsilon Pi, and Phi Alpha—took in many of the Jewish students, but there seemed something wrong in the fact that Jews were in a sort of ghetto in the university founded by America's leading champion of religious freedom and equality. This irony may have struck the non-Jewish students as strange as well, because in contrast to the evidence of social discrimination by fraternities, we find indications of full acceptance in other parts of university life.

In 1951 William L. Shapero was elected president of both the law school and the class of 1951, and as befitted an occupant of those positions, he became a member of Tilka, IMP, and the prestigious Thirteen Society. A few years later Thomas Hofheimer served as vice-president of the student council, treasurer of Skull & Keys, and a member of the Ravens, Omicron Delta Kappa, and the Thirteen Society. As the years went on, more and more Jewish students entered leadership roles in the university and found their efforts rewarded by induction into the honor societies as well as by securing prestigious rooms on the Lawn.

Unfortunately, the social discrimination evident at the university could be found elsewhere throughout the commonwealth. Although overt acts of anti-Semitism were rare, a more subtle form of prejudice led most of the better clubs and resorts in the state to close their doors to Jews, while certain neighborhoods were restricted. The Homestead, which Samuel Wurtzel had found so welcoming in the early 1930s, proved far less so in the 1940s. During the war an International Food Conference held there ignited a wave of adverse publicity when the hotel refused service to Jews and other minorities. Although Fay Ingalls, the president of the hotel, promised after that incident that the hotel would abandon its discriminatory policy, it did just the opposite. In 1944 Ingalls said he "would use every effort to discourage ... Jewish business." When a Dr. Blumstein of Philadelphia wrote requesting a reservation, he was turned down with a nasty anti-Semitic note. When his African-American maid, whose name sounded white and Protestant, wrote for a room, she received a confirmed reservation.

The Anti-Defamation League wrote to Abe Schewel, the owner of a large furniture store in Lynchburg (and whose son Elliot was elected time and again to the state Senate), and asked him if he could do something about the Homestead's policy. Schewel confirmed that the Homestead indeed discriminated and then wrote an eloquent letter to Fay Ingalls. Sometimes, Schewel wrote, he felt tired after working all week and liked to get away. In fact, many of his friends went to the Homestead and suggested that he join them. But he had learned that "you do not want any Jews at your hotel." Schewel continued:

> Surely I am a good citizen here. I have lived in Lynchburg fifty-nine years. I have tried to live a decent and respectable life and certainly could do no harm to your guests. I could converse with them on any average subject that they might bring up. I stay sober and attend to my own business and would not impose myself on any of your guests if I thought I was not welcome.
>
> There are hundreds of thousands of Jews like myself in America, decent, respectable people with the same culture and the same refinements and the same feeling and the same passions, the same likes and the same dislikes that Christians have. We have good people and bad people just like Christians have. As Christians, also, we have so many more good than bad.
>
> I cannot quite understand how you could feel this way to me, a perfect stranger to you, just because I am a Jew.

A few days later Schewel received a response from Ingalls. Although Ingalls noted that Schewel's letter "raises anew a question which has disturbed me deeply" and one "which goes to the very heart of our democratic way of life," he brushed off the issue as too complicated to be handled in a letter. Ingalls neither denied the discrimination nor suggested that the hotel had any intention of changing its policy. Only with the passage of the Civil Rights Act of 1964, with its requirement that public accommodations such as hotels and restaurants not discriminate on the basis of race or religion, did such overt policies finally pass from the scene. The exclusion of Jews in private clubs lingered much longer.

———

The national gratitude that enacted the G.I. Bill also made it possible for veterans to buy homes with little or no money down, thus bringing into the reach of millions what had previously been only a dream, owning one's home. Throughout America, the drive toward suburbia began, and in both larger cities as well as small towns, new homeowners strained existing communal resources. Within the Jewish community this building boom in the postwar years brought about the construction of many new synagogues as well as a new institution, the Jewish community center, which provided recreational and social resources for the population.

In October 1946, Richmond opened its new Jewish Center, a converted ten-room building on Idlewood Avenue, which had a gym, a library, and several meeting rooms or classrooms. It had been in operation less than two years when it burned. In 1949 the center bought the former Holy Comforter Episcopal Church on Grove Avenue. Within a decade, however, the demand of its membership for additional services and facilities had outgrown the center. In 1959 the trustees announced plans to raise the then unheard-of sum of $450,000 to build a brand new facility on ten acres off Monument Avenue in the West End, a building replete with an auditorium, game rooms, lounges, and a nursery school, and which would eventually expand to include an indoor swimming pool, gymnasium, and health club. Although built and maintained by funds from the Jewish community, the center has always been open to non-Jewish membership. Ironically, the owner of the land had not wanted to sell it to Jews, and so a front figure had made the initial purchase and then conveyed the site to the center.

Jewish community centers were built in other cities as well. Along with their construction came the establishment of new congregations, especially in the rapidly growing suburbs of northern Virginia, as well as the expansion of some older congregations. In Winchester, the small community decided in 1951 that it should build a synagogue and broke ground in the spring of 1954. The cost, which to the building committee seemed huge, came to $35,000. Although the Winchester community has lost population in recent years, in the 1950s and 1960s it had as many as forty children in the religious school and actually required an addition to the building.

In Lynchburg, the Jewish community grew to ninety families, and the Agudath Sholom synagogue of 1924, which many had thought would be all that the community would ever need, proved inadequate to the influx of new population. In 1953 the leaders of the congregation purchased eleven acres on Langhorne Road, the site of old Fort McCausland, where in 1864 Confederate forces had turned back Union troops in their assault on Lynchburg. Fund-raising for the new building went quickly amid the postwar prosperity, and the congregation held services in its new sanctuary on Rosh Hashanah 1956. (The old synagogue had been on Church Street, and when Agudath Sholom left that building, the street of churches no longer had any houses of worship on it.)

In Williamsburg, the number of Jewish families as well as Jewish students at the College of William and Mary had grown consistently. In 1959 Congregation Beth El began holding Friday night services in the college's historic Wren Building, which has been in continuous use since 1695, although never before, as far as anyone knew, had it been used as a synagogue. Although only a small congregation, Beth El soon needed a building of its own and took an unusual step in securing a facility. In 1968 Beth El purchased Mr. Foster's Remembrance Shop from Colonial Williamsburg and moved it to a vacant parcel it had purchased on Jamestown Road.

But if things seemed to be looking up for American Jewry after the war, European Jews who had survived had little to be optimistic about.

Liberated from the concentration camps, they had no place to go and soon wound up in Displaced Persons (DP) camps, where, even if not confronted with the threat of annihilation each day, they still found themselves confined and with little hope for the future. For many of them, their one dream lay in Palestine, where civil war between Jews, Arabs, and their British trustees seemed imminent.

Following V-E Day, Zionist groups had begun demanding that Great Britain open the gates of Palestine to Jews who had survived the Nazi death camps. The Labour government, however, had no sympathy for the Zionists and in effect repudiated the Balfour pledge of 1917; moreover, rather than admitting Jews, the United Kingdom seemed intent on keeping out those who wanted to enter, mainly in order to placate the Arabs, whose oil Britain badly needed.

In the United States, Zionist groups mounted an effective campaign to convince the public that not only should the gates of Palestine be open to the survivors, but that Britain should also leave and let those who lived in the Holy Land govern themselves. The seeming justice of this demand, a home for those the Nazis had made homeless, won over many Americans, Jew and Christian alike, and various groups put a great deal of pressure on the Truman administration to support this policy.

As the drive for a Jewish state picked up steam, American Jews did what they could to help. They sent supplies and money to the Haganah, the Jewish underground that fought first the British, and then after the British left in early 1948, the Arabs, until an independent Israel came into being. Much of this support had to be secret, because American laws prohibited the shipment of arms or war surplus goods overseas without a license, and one could not get a license to sell or ship to the Haganah.

One of the most important items supplied to the struggle had a definite Virginia connection. The Old Bay Line ran steamboats along the East Coast from 1840 to 1940, and one of the four pioneer steamboats had, in fact, been called the *Jewess*. Whether the owners remembered that or not, they could hardly have known in 1927 when they commissioned a 320-foot passenger and freight steamer to make the run between Baltimore and Norfolk how important that ship would be in Jewish affairs.

Named the *President Warfield* after the recently deceased president of the line, she served grandly until World War II, when the United States government took the vessel over and converted her to a troop carrier; despite some close calls, the *Warfield* came through the war unscathed. Decommissioned in September 1945, she was towed up the James and moored with the so-called Idle Fleet until sold to the Potomac Shipwrecking Company of Washington, which two days later passed her on at a tidy profit to the Weston Trading Company of New York, a front organization for the Haganah.

Mariners' Museum, Newport News

The *President Warfield*, a ship in the James River Reserve Fleet, became the *Exodus 1947*, used in an unsuccessful attempt to transport Jewish refugees from postwar Europe to Israel.

The new owners registered the ship, secretly fitted out to carry refugees, in Honduras, and she set sail supposedly to join the China trade. In fact, she went to the French port of Sette, where she took on 4,500 refugees and a new name, *Exodus 1947*, and steamed toward Palestine. British intelligence had learned of the planned rescue, and a destroyer accompanied the ship while she was in international waters. The British refused to allow the *Exodus 1947* to land, and when the crew tried to make a run for the shore, the British boarded and disabled her. The 4,500 passengers were put on three "prison" ships and taken back to Hamburg, amid howls of protest from all over the world. The *Exodus 1947* may have failed in her attempt to bring refugees to the Promised Land, but the uproar the mission aroused contributed immeasurably to the growing public support for an independent Jewish state.

It is safe to say that the vast majority of Jews within Virginia, as in the country as a whole, supported the drive for a Jewish state. But one group of Jews, the American Council for Judaism, strenuously opposed it, and in Virginia the council not only had some of its most loyal supporters but also some of its most eloquent champions.

The council grew out of classic Reform's opposition to Zionism and its belief that Judaism should not include any desire to reestablish a homeland in Palestine. In the 1930s, though, Zionism began to attract followers, especially when it became clear that refugees from fascism had few places to relocate. As a result, many Reform rabbis began to rethink the Pittsburgh platform and its overt and unyielding opposition to Zionism. In 1937 the Columbus platform stressed that all Jews had the obligation to aid in the rebuilding of Palestine both as a haven for the oppressed and as a center for Jewish self-renewal. A new generation born in America had entered the rabbinate, and they did not share the fears of dual loyalty that marked those who had come to maturity before World War I.

When the American Jewish Conference met in the middle of the Second World War and endorsed the Zionist call for a Jewish state in Palestine, that proved too much for those advocates of classic Reform who still adhered to the spirit of the 1885 document. One group of Reform rabbis, mainly from the southern and western states, formed the American Council for Judaism in August 1943, with the express purpose of fighting what they saw as the Zionist threat both to Judaism and to the status of American Jewry. Rabbi Edward N. Calisch of Richmond's Beth Ahabah stood as one of the most prominent members of the council and as one of the most vociferous opponents of Zionism, which he considered "misrepresentative" of Judaism. One of Calisch's most ardent supporters was Malcolm Stern, then in Philadelphia, but who moved to Norfolk to head the Reform congregation Ohef Sholom from 1947 to 1964.

Calisch in the period from 1943 to his death three years later did all he could to support the council and fight Zionism. He invited the executive director of the council to Richmond and personally solicited memberships from more than fifty congregants of Beth Ahabah. He distributed anti-Zionist tracts to members of the Richmond Area Clergy Association and to the press, but he hung back when some members of his congregation wanted to withdraw from the communal welfare drive, some of the proceeds of which were destined for Palestine.

The anxieties of council members now seem unreal and even at that time did not make sense to the majority of American Jews. The council feared that Christian neighbors would see Jews as loyal to the state in Palestine and not to America. Although a few anti-Semites have raised this charge, most Americans have seen it as perfectly natural that American Jews would want to help their co-religionists, first to establish a Jewish homeland and then to sustain it. They knew that American Jewry had no intention of moving to Israel or becoming Israeli citizens, and they saw support for the Jewish state as a unique form of philanthropy.

As early as 1927 the *Richmond News Leader* had called the Zionist settlements in Palestine "A Land of Idealists" and praised the accomplishments of the settlers in building Tel Aviv and reclaiming the desert for agriculture. The United Palestine Appeal, the editors concluded, deserved the support of all people who believed in dreams. Two decades later, the

OFF ON A FLYING MISSION—Rabbi Jonah B. Wise, national chairman of the United Jewish appeal, bids farewell in New York to Philip W. Klaus, of Richmond, who was selected by the Richmond Jewish Community Council to make a flying survey of the rehabilitation needs of Jews in Europe.

Klaus En Route to Germany After Conference in Paris

Philip W. Klaus, of 6105 Wesley Rd., Richmond, was en route to Germany today after conferring with Jefferson A. Caffery, United States ambassador to France, regarding the rehabilitation needs of the remaining Jews in Europe. The report on the trip was received here from Paris.

Mr. Klaus and 34 other American Jewish leaders are making a four-week flying tour of France, Germany, Italy and Palestine in conjunction with the $250,000,000 campaign of the United Jewish Appeal.

While in Germany the delegation is scheduled to confer with General Lucius D. Clay, United States military commander in Germany, and to inspect displaced persons' camps in Central Germany.

At a special reception at the America nembassy in Paris, Mr. Caffery said:

"I am very pleased to receive and extend my best wishes to the United Jewish Appeal delegation. I know that the reports these distinguished American Jewish community leaders will take back to America will be an inspiration for the great humanitarian work they are undertaking for their coreligionists overseas. I wish them every success in this great under-taking to alleviate human suffering."

The ambassador asked Mr. Klaus to impress upon the people of Richmond the urgency of the needs of the Jews of Europe that must be met this year.

During his four-day stay in France, the Richmonder visited hospitals, orphanages, training centers and other installations operated with funds raised by previous United Jewish Appeals.

Justice Miller to Talk

Justice Willis D. Miller, of the Supreme Court of Appeals, will address the McNeill Law Society of the University of Richmond Law School tonight at 8 o'clock. His topic will be trial techniques. In addition to Justice Miller's talk, the students will hear Judge Daniel G. Joyce, of Bassett, give an opinion on a moot case argued at the December meeting of the society.

The Richmond Jewish Community Federation chose Philip W. Klaus to make a survey of the rehabilitation needs of European Jews in 1948.

Richmond Times-Dispatch

paper endorsed the report of the Anglo-American Committee that 100,000 Jews should be immediately admitted to Palestine and called the proposal "Fair, therefore Acceptable." Shortly afterward the editors endorsed the annual United Jewish Appeal, which included funds for Palestine, and stated, "We are not content to wish them well in so sacred a venture; they deserve the prayers, the gifts, the cooperation of all Richmond, all Virginia."

Far more typical of Virginia Jewry's response to the creation of Israel were the thousands of men and women who made substantial donations to the United Jewish Appeal and to special campaigns to aid the enterprise. Some did more. The Richmond Jewish Community Federation wanted to know exactly what conditions were like in the Displaced Persons (DP) camps of Europe and in Palestine in the winter of 1948, the time between the United Nations vote on the partition of Palestine in November 1947 and the scheduled end of the British mandate the following May. The community leaders asked businessman Philip W. Klaus to go on a four-week United Jewish Appeal mission, during which he visited the camps, met with European and American officials, and then went on to Palestine. In Europe he saw "the misery and the suffering of thousands of innocent people and especially children," but what impressed him most was "the dignity, the courage, and the unbreakable spirit of the average Jewish D.P."

Klaus, a member of Beth Ahabah, wrote to his family how he had been "adopted" by the St. Louis delegation, a number of whose members were of eastern European origin and spoke Yiddish, which he described "as the mother tongue of the D.P." Their translations of the questioning opened up a new world for him. "No experience that I have ever had can approach this trip," he confided. "It has been an education in itself, and one that touches the field of politics, sociology, and all phases of human relations. I have been fortunate."

The camps showed Klaus and the other delegates the problem; when they got to Palestine, they saw the solution. Whatever views the American Council for Judaism (of which Klaus was then a member) had tried to propagate vanished in the face of the reality of the Jewish settlements and the stark contrast of free Jews living in a land of their own and those still huddled behind the barbed wire fences of the DP camps. Klaus spoke glowingly to reporters after he returned from his visit to a kibbutz, a communal agricultural settlement, which in sixteen years had taken a swamp and turned it into a productive farm and home for 850 people.

Klaus was also a realist, however, and he warned about the impending strife. "Anarchy will prevail as the British withdraw and one can predict the subsequent developments or the final outcome," he cautioned. That possibility, of course, was what worried Jews everywhere and had been the basis for the historic 1948 UJA campaign, which set out to raise the then unheard-of sum of $250 million. Communities like those in Richmond and Norfolk, as well as those in the smaller towns, had to understand what was at stake.

Klaus had paid for the trip out of his own pocket so he would not be influenced by the views of the sponsoring agencies. Moreover, he had departed on the mission as a staunch supporter of Calisch, but what he saw on the tour completely changed his views. In the weeks following his return, he helped open the eyes of other Virginians.

The money raised by the campaign, which exceeded its goal, helped the Jews of Palestine establish Israel and secure the arms needed to win the War for Independence in 1948. Next, a country had to be created, one that immediately opened its doors to accept the DPs that no other country would take. Arthur Taubman, a Roanoke businessman, then president of Advance Stores (which sold automobile accessories in four states and is now called Advance Auto Parts, with stores in many states), wanted to help. He and a friend, A. L. Friedlander of the Dayton Rubber Company, visited Israel in 1949, when the scars of the War for Independence were still quite visible. They realized that the new state needed more than just charity; it needed factories and jobs so that it could build up its economy.

They arranged a contract with Histadrut, Israel's general labor federation, a workers' cooperative that runs everything from dairies to a health plan, to build a tire factory at Hadera, midway between the two port cities of Tel Aviv and Haifa. The plant was capitalized at $2.9 million, half of which was put up by Histadrut and the other half raised in the United States. Taubman set about selling the stock. He told people he met at parlor meetings, "This thing is an investment. It has overtones that might involve a loss. If you're just a businessman, then invest your money in [the United States]. But if you're 75 percent business and 25 percent emotion, then invest in Israel." Six hundred investors took stock in the Alliance Tire and Rubber Co., Ltd., and Taubman's friend Friedlander provided the technical advice to get the company started. It began operations in September 1952 and lost $33,000 the first four months; after that, it ran at a profit. In his office in Staunton, Taubman kept a big truck tire, with Hebrew letters stamped into the side reading "Made in Israel."

Another important Virginia connection to the new state could be found in the Levinson Livestock Company of Newport News. As part of its efforts to help Europe recover from World War II, the United Nations Relief and Rehabilitation Agency (UNRRA) had begun a program of shipping livestock to Europe to help restock the farms devastated by the war. Between 1948 and 1952, tens of thousands of heads of cattle and horses made their way over the Chesapeake & Ohio system to Newport News, where Ben and Sol Levinson shipped most of them to Europe. Many, however, were sent to the new State of Israel, where they were distributed to the kibbutzim and moshavim as both breeding and work animals.

With more and more American Jews supporting the State of Israel, the American Council for Judaism almost collapsed after 1948, but a hard-core group remained, determined to fight what it considered a betrayal of Judaism and Americanism. Many of the council members whom Calisch had recruited refused for a number of years to give to the United Jewish Appeal or, if they did so, insisted that none of their contribution went to help Israel. As late as 1972, officers of the council, which by then had relatively few members, wrote long letters to the *Richmond Times-Dispatch* rehearsing the familiar themes that not all Jews are Zionists and that the Israelis had pulled the propaganda shades down over the eyes of America. In 1974 Virginia Commonwealth University hired a new head of its history

Israeli prime minister David Ben-Gurion observed the first tires made at the American-financed tire plant in Hadera in 1952.

department who had written widely on American Zionism. He gave a Friday night talk at Beth Ahabah on the subject, and several of the older members who had at one time been or still were affiliated with the council complained to the rabbi about the presentation.

Although there may still be some Jews who remain committed to the council's ideology, they are few and far between, even in southern states such as Virginia, which provided the bulk of the council's finances and membership. Following the wars against Israel in 1967 and 1973, the Jewish communities of Virginia, like their counterparts around the country, united in defense of the Jewish state and joined to raise as much money as they could to meet the emergency. The Israeli victories brought pride to the communities. "Israel has brought Jews up off their knees onto two feet," a pawnshop owner in Southside Virginia declared. "For the first time, I feel more like a tank commander than a suffering old Jew. We'll whip the Russians and the Egyptians, too, if we have too." The leading politician in Virginia, Senator Harry Flood Byrd, Sr., agreed. Always a staunch supporter of the Jewish state, Byrd and such fellow southerners as Herman Talmadge and Strom Thurmond used their considerable influence in the Senate to secure military aid for Israel.

In 1954 Jewish communities around Virginia and the nation celebrated the tercentenary of Jewish settlement in the United States. Although Jews had been in Virginia from the time of its settlement, the arrival of twenty-three Jews in New Amsterdam in September 1654 and the establishment of a community there marks the formal beginning of American Jewish history.

Each state had a committee to arrange events. Saul Viener of Richmond, later a president of the American Jewish Historical Society, coordinated the festivities in Virginia, while another Virginian, Samuel Binswanger, served on the national committee. The year-long celebration included an exhibit of costumes, portraits, manuscripts, and ceremonial objects at the Valentine Museum in Richmond; a drama, *Under Freedom*, portraying Jewish life in America; and, to end the year, the rededication of the 165-year-old Franklin Street burying ground, which included the laying of a wreath by the Daughters of the American Revolution in honor of Jacob I. Cohen, a Revolutionary War soldier.

Even as Virginia Jews wrestled with the problems of a Jewish state and celebrated the tercentenary, they became caught up in what has been the major social controversy of the later twentieth century, the effort to resolve racial injustice in a nation committed to democratic ideals. In May 1954, the United States Supreme Court handed down its decision in the school

Peninsula Jewish Historical Society

Under the auspices of the United Nations Relief and Rehabilitation Agency, Ben and Sol Levinson, owners of one of the largest cattle and hog feedlot operations in Virginia, contracted with the federal government to export livestock to Europe from the Newport News terminal to replenish those animals destroyed during World War II. Ben Levinson said, "We had the facilities. We shipped 146,000 cattle to Europe. It was more than all other U.S. ports put together." The new State of Israel was another major destination for Levinson Livestock Company.

Courtesy of Robert P. Frank

Harry and Lilyan M. Frank of Newport News instilled in their sons the values of duty and public service. Robert P. Frank (left) became a judge of the Newport News circuit court; his brother, Joe S. (second from the right), was elected mayor.

desegregation cases, consolidated in *Brown* v. *Board of Education*, and ruled that segregation based on race violated the equal protection clause of the Fourteenth Amendment.

Although national Jewish groups such as B'nai B'rith's Anti-Defamation League, the American Jewish Committee, and the American Jewish Congress had all taken strong stands on civil rights, the southern chapters had been very quiet. Southern Jews shared many of the prejudices of other whites and believed in segregation. Even those sympathetic to the plight of African Americans feared that a backlash would include Jews as well as blacks, and to some extent their fears proved well grounded. To give but one example, the University of Virginia found swastikas painted on the walls of Old Cabell with the slogan "Jews—Back to Your Homeland" after B'nai B'rith called for racial integration of the nation's colleges and universities.

The Anti-Defamation League (ADL) in 1954 maintained an office in Richmond that covered all of Virginia and North Carolina. Its main purpose was and always has been to combat anti-Semitism. In the early 1950s many exclusive clubs had closed their doors to Jews, and some resorts had openly advertised that they did not take Jewish clients. The local ADL, headed by Samuel Binswanger and which included many of the state's leading Jews, had just successfully lobbied the Virginia General Assembly to enact legislation, aimed primarily at Virginia Beach and hotels such as the Cavalier, banning discriminatory religious advertising. The Richmond office, in cooperation with the local chapter of the National Conference of Christians and Jews, also sponsored an all-day youth seminar each summer that brought together black and white high school seniors to discuss how different groups could learn to live together.

In July 1954, the ADL sent a new regional director to Richmond. Murray Friedman was a son of eastern European immigrants who had grown up in Brooklyn amid Orthodox Jews, a graduate of Brooklyn College, and as he later described himself, "idealistic and not a little unworldly." He unknowingly walked into a hornet's nest and soon found himself caught between the local leadership, which wanted to avoid taking any stand on racial matters, and the national office, which strongly supported the ruling in *Brown*.

It was an impossible task, because bigots found it convenient to try to make Jews scapegoats for the racial crisis confronting the South. Anti-Semitic literature flooded into Virginia, and before long *The Virginian*, published in Newport News, poured out vicious tirades against Jews and Judaism. *The Virginian* went after Friedman and the ADL. The paper charged that Jews wanted to "mongrelize" the white race. In fact, because of pressure from his local board, Friedman had kept a fairly low profile on racial matters and had tried to focus on the ADL's traditional target, anti-Semitism. Many people, however, did not bother to distinguish between national and local agencies, and the fact that the ADL's national office supported desegregation was all that mattered.

On 7 July 1958, James J. Kilpatrick, the editor of the *Richmond News Leader* and one of the most outspoken foes of desegregation, published an editorial that reverberated throughout the commonwealth. Apparently triggered by the Richmond office of the ADL's distribution of literature promoting a workshop on integration sponsored by the NAACP, the editorial, entitled "Anti-Semitism in the South," asked why there had been so many recent manifestations of this prejudice. "This is a new thing," Kilpatrick wrote. "We are strangers to it. A South that has honored [Bernard] Baruch and [Lewis L.] Strauss, and placed a Judah P. Benjamin on the Confederate Cabinet, knows nothing of anti-semitism."

Temple Beth-El, Richmond

Albert Furman, president of Temple Beth-El, hosted Governor Thomas B. Stanley and his wife, Anne Pocahontas Bassett Stanley, at a congregational seder in the mid-1950s. The seder, a service including a ceremonial meal, is held on the first evening of Passover and commemorates the freeing of the Jewish slaves from bondage in Egypt as told in the book of Exodus.

Kilpatrick ignored the fact that nearly all of the major country clubs and resort hotels around the state, including the Country Club of Virginia in Richmond, the Farmington in Charlottesville, the Homestead, and the Cavalier, routinely excluded Jews, while many of the better residential neighborhoods were restricted to white, Anglo-Saxon Protestants.

Pointing to the distribution of the NAACP material, the editorial asserted that the actions of the local branch of B'nai B'rith were "identifying all Jewry with the advocacy of compulsory integration." Kilpatrick acknowledged that in a free country, the ADL had a right to say what it wanted, but he warned that "militancy invites retaliation." Relations between Jews and gentiles were "excellent in the South before the ADL began setting up regional offices, as in Richmond, and stirring up clouds of prejudice and misunderstanding." On a not-too-subtle note, Kilpatrick suggested that some of the area's leading Jews look into the matter and stop it at once.

The editorial touched a nerve throughout the city, the commonwealth, and beyond, as it was picked up, reprinted, and circulated throughout the South. Supporters of massive resistance had a new villain in their cast of characters and could blame the Jews as well as the Supreme Court for their troubles. A young Jewish attorney in Roanoke was discussing school desegregation with a non-Jewish friend, when the latter remarked, "I hear that the president of the NAACP is Jewish." Within a day everyone in the Jewish community had heard the story, and the next day a call was made to discover the truth of the charge. When Virginians learned that Arthur B. Spingarn, a New York Jew, was indeed the president of the NAACP, there was a grim silence at the southern end of the telephone line.

How in fact did Virginia Jews feel about desegregation? Friedman believed that more than other whites, Jews sympathized with African Americans who suffered from prejudice, a condition not unknown in Jewish history. "But," he argued, "they are unwilling to set themselves off from the dominant white majority, to which they have made such strenuous efforts to belong. So they keep their views to themselves—which causes further uneasiness." Stephen Whitfield has suggested that relations between Jews and gentiles in the South had been excellent as long as Jews did not take seriously the prophetic injunction of "justice, justice shalt thou pursue." This holding back was "the poignant price Southern Jewry was expected to pay in order to get along with their neighbors," and as events showed, the seemingly good relations could easily fall victim to the passions of racism.

The fact of increased anti-Semitism could not be ignored. Although there were no temple bombings in the Old Dominion as there were in Atlanta, the amount of hate literature circulating around the state increased from practically nothing to a raging torrent. Anti-Semitic pamphlets and letters went to seniors at high schools in Arlington. In Norfolk and Newport News, business and professional people received letters postmarked Los Angeles carrying literature published by Frank Britton, editor of the virulently racist *American Nationalist*. Just before school opened in the fall of 1958, an estimated 15,000 pieces of hate literature were distributed door-to-door in Norfolk. The February–March 1958 publication of the Defenders of State Sovereignty and Individual Liberties, one of the three leading segregationist groups in the state, carried a picture of Thurgood Marshall, the NAACP lead counsel in *Brown*, receiving a plaque from Kivie Kaplan of Boston, described as the co-chair of the NAACP Life Membership Committee, and Arthur Spingarn, the NAACP president. The caption read, "THE NAACP IS NOT A NEGRO ORGANIZATION AND NEVER HAS BEEN." A pamphlet put out by the Defenders called for Anglo-Saxon "racial purity" and attacked the "agitarian Jews" who were solely responsible for the Marxist campaign to undermine the white race.

In the face of such an attack, most moderate Jews, like most moderate Christians, retreated into a shell of silence. A few, a very few, tried to do something, and one can only regret that men and women of goodwill, Christian as well as Jew, were intimidated into silence. There were a few exceptions.

Irving Held, an insurance agent, belonged to the Richmond First Club, a group of businessmen described by one source as "reasonably successful in their businesses who were an integral part of the business community, social life of the community, in fact, in all aspects of the community." It was also a moderate group, concerned that continued resistance to desegregation would be futile and would hurt the city's and the state's economy. If desegregation was going to come then, as Held put it, "let's do it with the least disruption as possible."

Held and other members of Richmond First labored quietly for six months trying to come up with alternatives to massive resistance. The committee concluded that "integration of the public schools of Richmond could proceed smoothly if parents and officials would resolve to make it work." These words of reason perhaps swayed some other moderates, but the report and the voices of moderation were drowned out, at least temporarily, by those chanting, "Never." As one student of the period commented, the "findings of the report were at least ten years too early for Richmond's consideration."

In Norfolk, Congregation Ohef Sholom offered the use of its facilities to the school board when massive resistance forced the closing of schools in that city. Believing that a majority of people in the city opposed massive resistance, Rabbi Malcolm Stern publicly urged a referendum on the closings.

Ohef Sholom, in fact, had been ahead of its time in its attitude toward blacks. In 1951 Temple University's racially diverse A Capella Choir had performed in Norfolk at Ohef Sholom. After the performance, one of the congregation's members informed Ruth Sinberg, a young white singer from Pennsylvania, that this had been the first time that black attendees at an event in the synagogue had been seated on the main floor of the sanctuary instead of being relegated to the balcony.

Many of the Jews who lived in northern Virginia had migrated from northern states after World War II and worked for the federal government and thus were immune to the social and economic pressure that could be applied against moderates in Richmond, Norfolk, and elsewhere in the state. In Alexandria's Beth El, the third oldest congregation in the commonwealth, Rabbi Emmet A. Frank delivered a blistering Yom Kippur sermon on 25 September 1958 entitled "Byrdliness versus Godliness." Frank denounced massive resistance and those "vocal segregationists who for a few moments of political glory have placed in jeopardy our nation." The rabbi did not mince words; he identified the "Byrd oligarchy" as the chief cause of the state's troubles and denounced its policy as one of "godlessness."

He also warned that the commonwealth's Jews could not "remain silent to social injustice against anyone. The fresh wounds of Hitlerism, the ghettos of Europe ... these are the results of silence." He cited the prophets Amos and Malachi in their call for justice and also looked to Thomas Jefferson, whom he held up as a model for all Virginians.

The sermon, as strong a statement by a white minister against massive resistance and segregation as can be found any place in the history of the civil rights movement, predictably aroused the bigots, who sent threatening and hateful mail. There were also expressions of concern that such a sermon seemed "inappropriate" coming from a rabbi, and on Yom Kippur at that. Within the congregation some members objected. A few members strongly backed the Byrd Organization and massive resistance; others feared controversy, which they worried would create ill feeling between Jews and their Christian neighbors. The majority of the congregation, however, supported not only their rabbi's controversial statement but also his right to say it, to jostle the consciences of the people on a day when each Jew is expected to look inside himself or herself and evaluate how he or she has lived in the preceding year.

The sermon quickly attracted attention throughout the nation. Richmond and Danville newspapers attacked Frank for placing Byrd in the ranks of the godless, while the *Washington Post* commended his courage. Within Alexandria, eleven Christian ministers came to his defense. Then on 19 October 1958, just before Frank was to speak at Arlington's Unitarian Church, its minister, the Reverend Allen Weston, asked the congregation to leave quietly; an anonymous caller had warned that the church would be bombed.

Churches and synagogues had already been bombed in other parts of the South, but Virginia had so far been spared the violence. This threat finally brought some people back to their senses. Governor J. Lindsay Almond, Jr., assailed the vicious cranks who would stoop to such action, and many of the state's newspapers also joined in the denunciation.

Gradually the crisis passed, not only in Alexandria, where the incident strengthened relations between Jews and Christians, but in the state as well. Massive resistance collapsed, and eventually all of the legal supports for segregation fell. Although the goals of a true integration have yet to be achieved, the fury that accompanied events in the 1950s and 1960s passed, and Virginia's Jewry moved on to other matters.

The turmoil of the civil rights movement, the women's movement, and opposition to the war in Vietnam all predictably triggered a conservative

Beth El Hebrew Congregation Archives, Alexandria

A bomb threat was called in to the Unitarian church in Arlington when Rabbi Emmet A. Frank of Beth El in Alexandria was scheduled to speak on 19 October 1958. Earlier, Frank, who favored integration and an end to massive resistance, had delivered a sermon entitled "Byrdliness versus Godliness."

backlash to the liberalism of the 1960s. One aspect of this conservatism that Jews found particularly troubling was the rise of a militant Christian social conservatism that entered politics in a way no religious group had done in recent American history.

Neither Jerry Falwell's Moral Majority in the 1980s nor Pat Robertson's Christian Coalition in the 1990s has been overtly anti-Semitic. In fact, both groups have proven strong supporters of Israel on theological grounds, partly because they believe that the ingathering of the Jews to their ancient homeland is a precondition for the second coming of Christ. Unfortunately, some of their followers have been less charitable.

In August 1980, the Reverend Bailey Smith, president of the 13.8 million–member Southern Baptist Convention, declared that God does not hear the prayers of Jews. This sentiment was then repeated in modified form in October at a regional meeting of the National Religious Broadcasters by televangelist Jerry Falwell of Lynchburg, who declared that God hears only the prayers of "redeemed Gentiles and Jews," and who went on to define "redeemed" as "one who trusts in God through his faith in Jesus

Christ." Falwell tried to tone down the statement afterward by noting that it was only his theological belief and said that a rabbi "may not think a Baptist's prayer is heard by God," while fundamentalists believe only a Christian's prayer is heard.

The so-called Christian Right has also announced its goal, as Pat Robertson put it, to "establish a Christian United States," a sentiment echoed by other fundamentalist leaders, including Falwell. Few have been quite so blunt as Randall Terry, founder of Operation Rescue, who declared: "Our goal is a Christian nation. We have a biblical duty, we are called by God, to conquer this country. We don't want equal time. We don't want pluralism."

Falwell's comments were quickly attacked, not only by Jews but by some Christians as well, including two prominent Baptist ministers in Richmond, Dr. Luther Joe Thomson of the First Baptist Church and the Reverend James Slatton of the River Road Church, Baptist. Moreover, when Ronald Reagan, then the Republican presidential candidate, came to speak to conservative religious broadcasters in Lynchburg, he declared that the "God of Moses" hears everyone's prayers.

The rise of the Christian Right troubles not only Jews but many Christians as well, and in Virginia there is a certain irony to the fact that the state that is home to both Falwell and Robertson is also the state where Thomas Jefferson and James Madison first established the principle of religious freedom and equality.

"A PART BUT NOT APART"

In October 1976, a group of scholars and interested lay persons under the auspices of the American Jewish Historical Society met in Richmond at Virginia Commonwealth University to reconstitute a Southern Jewish Historical Society. One had been started several years earlier but had failed to make a place for itself. The keynote speaker at the gathering was Eli N. Evans, author of *The Provincials: A Personal History of Jews in the South* (1973), who noted that the dilemma of southern Jews has been "to be a part but not to be apart." They have been "a blood-and-bones part of the South itself . . . passing for white in that mysterious underland of America." By this he meant that although Jews had been part of the southern fabric for centuries, they had always been concerned about being accepted. In part their acceptance had been made easier by the presence of blacks, who served as the traditional lightning rod for local prejudice. "With the end of isolation and the arrival of the South into the nation," argued Evans, "it is easier to be Jewish in the South."

Evans's comments surely resonate among the Jews of Virginia. They have been, as he noted, "a blood-and-bones part" of the commonwealth's history, going all the way back to that first ill-fated Roanoke expedition. They have fought in all of its wars, they have served the state in various capacities, and their economic prosperity has been closely bound up with that of Virginia. They have shared the joys and sorrows, the triumphs and tribulations of the Old Dominion.

They have been a part and most of the time not apart, yet there have been instances of anti-Semitism. There have been times when Jews could not help but be a little bit apart. The traumas of the 1950s and 1960s exacerbated that sense. But as Virginia prepares for its 400th anniversary, the Jews of Virginia not only feel more at home, more a part of the commonwealth, but also believe that their neighbors more than at any other time in their history understand and accept that as a minority with a history going back four thousand years, Jews may at times have to stand a little bit apart.

On Yom Kippur 1973, one of the holiest days in the Jewish calendar, Egypt and Syria launched a sneak attack on Israel, and for the first few days

Peninsula Jewish Historical Society

Newport News elected its first Jewish member of the Virginia House of Delegates, Alan A. Diamonstein, in 1967.

of the war many people wondered if the Jewish state would survive. At the same time, Arab states in the United Nations, as well as some leftist groups in the United States, launched a new form of anti-Semitism by denouncing Zionism as racism. For those familiar with Israeli history, the charges could be shrugged off as hateful propaganda. But what about those who did not know much about Israel? What could be done to teach them, not only about Israel, but also about its importance to Jews everywhere?

The answer in Virginia proved to be the Israeli Showcase, the product of two years' labor by hundreds of people in Richmond and across the state. The idea of converting the Richmond Jewish Community Center into Jerusalem for one week came out of a small group of communal leaders who met over lunch one day, decided to do it, and drafted Neil November to coordinate what proved to be the most massive single project in Virginia Jewish history.

There had been a few similar projects elsewhere, but they were usually undertaken by larger communities. In fact, during the planning stages for the Virginia project, the St. Louis community mounted such an event. The planning committee, in a plane offered for its use by the Reverend Jerry Falwell, flew out to Missouri to see what had been done, what not to do, and what it could do differently.

For the next eighteen months, hundreds of volunteers labored on different aspects of the Showcase. In a northside warehouse models of streets, the tomb of Christ, and other parts of the Holy City were built. The cultural affairs committee worked to bring in performing artists and to set

The Israeli Showcase in 1976 turned Richmond's Jewish Community Center into Jerusalem for a week.

Richmond Times-Dispatch

Governor Mills E. Godwin, Jr., lit a menorah taper with Neil November, general chairman of the Israeli Showcase, at the opening ceremonies.

up the largest single exhibit of Israeli art ever seen in the United States in one place.

The back wall of the center was covered with plastic stones that looked exactly like the Western Wall, the one wall remaining of Solomon's Temple. In one part of the center, the Street of Chains and a *shuk* (market) were recreated. Outside, the volunteers built a kibbutz, where area Boy Scouts camped out alongside Israeli Scouts during the week. A facsimile of the Dead Sea Scrolls as well as an archaeological dig, complete with a mummy, proved to be popular attractions. Every night a different activity highlighted some aspect of Israeli life and culture—a fashion show, a dance performance, a play, or a concert.

November got the help of practically the entire community. The local Coca-Cola distributor ran off bottles similar to those produced in Israel, with the familiar Coke logo in Hebrew letters. Merchants threw in enormous amounts of free publicity by adding information on the Showcase to their advertisements in the newspapers. November made sure that area churches understood that this was not just a Jewish showcase but was intended to instruct visitors about Jerusalem and Israel, a city and a land holy to three faiths. (After the end of the Showcase, the model of Christ's tomb found a permanent home in the Greek Orthodox church.)

On 15 May, despite threatening gray skies, more than 5,600 people showed up for the opening ceremonies, including Governor Mills E. Godwin, Jr., Senator Harry F. Byrd, Jr., and a host of other dignitaries. Over the next week some 40,000 Virginians visited the Showcase, ate Israeli food, watched Israeli performers, bought Israeli-made goods, and joined one of the various prayer sessions at "The Wall."

The *Richmond Times-Dispatch* congratulated the sponsors on what had been a dazzling event and said they deserved the "thanks of the entire community," not only for emphasizing the achievements of Israel but also for rekindling "an interest in Richmonders of diverse faiths in their own ancestral links to the cradle of civilization in the Middle East."

Following the establishment of the State of Israel, the subject of the Holocaust disappeared for a number of years from public discussion. Even among Jews it was seldom mentioned, and the survivors of the camps also seemed to prefer silence. Israelis did create Yad Vashem in Jerusalem, a combination memorial, museum, and research library that over the years has achieved the status of a quasi-religious site. But in the United States there were no books, no plays, no television shows, no courses in universities.

That lack of emphasis slowly began to change following the capture of Adolf Eichmann in 1960 and his public trial in Israel the following year, but even then, much of the discussion took place *en famille*, as survivors slowly began speaking about their experiences. But it spread, as the non-Jewish community sought to understand not only what had happened but also how and why. Since then the commemoration of the Holocaust has become a shared event, still primarily a Jewish mourning for six million victims, but also a community event in which non-Jews have expressed their grief.

One of the first of these events took place in Richmond in early October 1961, when an interfaith group, led by Beth Ahabah's rabbi, Ariel L. Goldburg, paid tribute to the heroism of Christians who had risked their lives to save Jews during the Second World War. Ernest M. Gunzberg, a German refugee who escaped in 1935, noted that "even in the darkest hours of the Nazi era, some stars shone: These were the stars of the Christian heroes who dared to act ingeniously, helping their Jewish brothers survive."

Soon a Holocaust memorial day or week was established, marked by public programs in schools, in colleges, and in the community. In nearly all of these ceremonies Christians stood next to Jews, and very often the speakers, in addition to survivors, were public figures or officials. In 1982, for example, Governor Charles S. Robb and historian-editor Virginius Dabney addressed a somber Holocaust observance on the steps of the state capitol.

At the same time, nearly every college and university in the state began offering courses on the Holocaust, and often a majority of the students enrolled were not Jewish. Frequently these courses featured as guest speakers local people who had survived the camps and who told stunned audiences what it had been like in Auschwitz or Bergen-Belsen. The reason they finally came forward was captured by Bernard Cytryn, who survived some of the worst camps in eastern Europe: "Please make sure that this life story of me should not stay on the shelves and collect dust. Please pass it on. Let the future generations learn and know that a Holocaust did happen."

The public awareness of the Holocaust may explain in part the strong public support during the 1970s and 1980s given to groups working to get Jews out of Russia, where, despite communist claims to the contrary, Jews suffered severe restrictions reminiscent of tsarist times. Within Virginia, Jewish communities as well as individual synagogues sponsored Russian immigrants and helped them to settle into a new home much different from that they had known under the communists. Now these immigrants, like the Sephardim and the Germans and the eastern Europeans before them, are beginning to realize the promise of freedom. They have found jobs or started their own businesses. Just as the earlier waves of immigrants reinvigorated Virginia Jewry, so the new Virginians from Russia are helping contemporary congregations and communities.

———

The 1980s proved a time of great growth for Virginia Jewry. Aside from the new immigrants from the Soviet Union, many northerners moved South, not only to the older established communities of Richmond and Tidewater, but also to the burgeoning Washington suburbs in northern Virginia. Many of today's most vibrant congregations are less than thirty years old; their temples stand on land that only a few years ago was either farmland or forest. When Rodef Shalom in Falls Church broke ground for its new building, its members (many of whom had at one time belonged to Alexandria's Beth El) had to tramp along a woodland path to get to the site.

In 1985 two fledgling congregations, Ner Tamid of Woodbridge (founded by seven families in 1970) and Bayis Shalom of Manassas (founded in the home of one of its members in 1971), merged to form Congregation Ner

Temple Rodef Shalom, Falls Church

This protest in Lafayette Park, across from the White House, on behalf of Soviet Jewry included members of Temple Rodef Shalom in Falls Church.

Shalom of Woodbridge. Within five years, membership had grown to more than three hundred families, and in October 1993 the congregation broke ground for its new synagogue, which it dedicated just one year later.

On a cold February evening in 1986, Governor Gerald L. Baliles sat waiting in his capitol office for the legislature to finish its work and adjourn. Suddenly he got an idea and called in two of his aides, Jordan Goldman and Richard Arenstein. "In two years," he told them, "Israel will celebrate its fortieth anniversary. We can send a trade mission over at the time, but why don't we do something bigger than that?" The three men talked about what to do, and out of their discussions came the Virginia-Israel Commission, headed by the indefatigable Neil November.

Created by executive order on 14 May 1986, the commission was charged with exploring "the cultural, educational, and economic development opportunities between the Commonwealth of Virginia and the State of Israel, and to chart the Commonwealth's commemoration of Israel's fortieth anniversary." Jordan Goldman served as the vice-chair and the

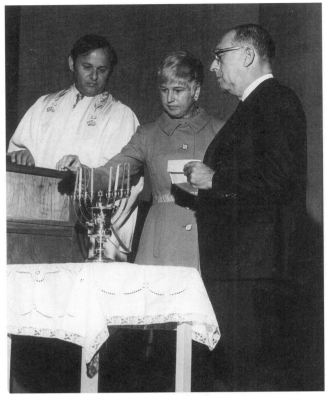

Rodef Shalom in Falls Church
held dedication services in
1970.

Temple Rodef Shalom, Falls Church

representative of the governor's office, while more than one hundred
people from all over the state were appointed to the commission. Thousands more volunteered and made the event a statewide undertaking.

November created twelve committees, with responsibilities in such areas
as agriculture, human and natural resources, science, education, tourism,
and economic development. Within each committee subcommittees set up
specific programs and exchanges. In one such exchange, the head archae-
ologist at Monticello spent three weeks in Israel working at sites that went
back not four hundred years but four thousand, while Israelis joined in
helping to excavate sites in the Old Dominion. They then shared ideas
about how different techniques might work in the two places.

Businesses were encouraged to set up ties, and the governor personally
led a large group of Virginia business officials to Israel to exchange
information on economic opportunities. At the 1988 Virginia Press Association meeting in Richmond, reporters from Israeli papers discussed issues
of mutual concern with their Virginia counterparts—privacy, censorship,
and dealing with government news sources.

Ronald E. Carrier, president of James Madison University, joined Israeli scientists at the Weizman Institute in a discussion of solar power, while the Medical College of Virginia's Cancer Center welcomed Israeli doctors working to fight the dread disease. At the College of William and Mary's law school, a conference that included Israeli Jews and Arabs, as well as leading American scholars, spent two days examining the growing phenomenon of religious fundamentalism around the world.

The exchanges involved people at every level, from junior high school on, Christians and Jews, blacks and whites, residents of the Tidewater, northern Virginia, the Valley, and the Richmond metropolitan area. Israel's famous Inbal dance troupe performed in Virginia, while artists from around the state journeyed to Jerusalem and Haifa and Tel Aviv to act, sing, and make music for Israeli audiences.

Baliles and November then led a gala mission to Israel, where they climbed Masada, toured the country, and placed a plaque commemorating the commission's work on a hilltop, over which flew the flags of Virginia and Israel. The tour ended with a festive dinner in the Great Hall of the Knesset, with the Marc Chagall tapestries as a backdrop. There Vice-Premier Shimon Peres praised the Virginia commission and its governor for their unique vision—"A pioneering idea from a pioneering state."

At least one project of the commission has had a lasting effect. Dr. Reuven Feuerstein, an Israeli psychologist, came to Lynchburg College at

Governor Gerald L. Baliles created the Virginia-Israel Commission by executive order in 1986 and named Neil November to chair it. On a visit to Israel the two placed a plaque commemorating the commission on a hilltop at Kiryat Menachem, over which flew the flags of Virginia and Israel.

Library of Virginia

This silver mezuzah is the work of Linda Gissen (b. 1937) of Richmond and, later, Virginia Beach. A container affixed to a doorpost, a mezuzah holds a *klaf*, a parchment containing verses from the Torah. The mezuzah serves two functions. First, it symbolizes to all who enter that this is a Jewish household with special rules and beliefs. Second, all Jews entering and leaving the room are reminded of the covenant they have with God.

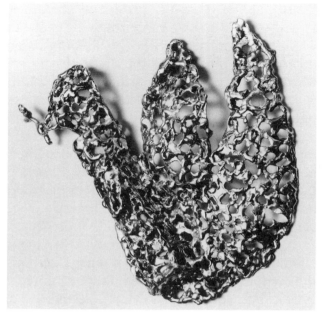

Beth Ahabah Museum and Archives

the invitation of the commission to talk about his unusual work with mentally retarded children. Since that time, a faculty member from Lynchburg College has gone to Israel every summer to study with Feuerstein and to teach in his international conference. There are also courses and summer institutes for teachers who want to learn his theories in central Virginia, and Lynchburg College is currently considering setting up a Reuven Feuerstein Center.

The Jewish experience in Virginia is a long one, but it is a story that is just beginning to be told. The growth of the state in the last two decades has seen a new migration of Jews into the commonwealth, until the Jewish population now totals about 70,000, with roughly half that number living in northern Virginia. Like previous newcomers, the current wave has added immeasurably to the welfare and prosperity of the Old Dominion. If the great department stores founded in the nineteenth century are no longer with us, new businesses—such as Circuit City, S&K, and Advance Auto Parts—have taken their place.

Many of the old congregations such as Beth El, Ohef Sholom, and Beth Ahabah have been reinvigorated by new members, while in other places, especially northern Virginia, a host of new and vibrant congregations have sprung up not only to serve their members' needs but also to "seek the peace of the city" as they participate in interfaith social welfare programs.

At the state's colleges and universities one finds Jewish students and faculty members, and there are programs in Judaic studies at nearly every major school. Jewish doctors, lawyers, engineers, city council members, mayors, assemblymen, government officials, business leaders, and teachers are found throughout the state, integral parts of Virginia life.

A close examination will uncover problems confronting Virginia's Jews. Intermarriage and resulting assimilation is a worry, as it is to Jews throughout the free world. There are still vestiges of social discrimination and an occasional outburst of vandalism or swastika painting, but these are universally condemned and, fortunately, are the exception rather than the rule. The freedom that Jews sought in coming to the New World is to be found in the Old Dominion, hallowed by the efforts of Thomas Jefferson, James Madison, and others. The Jewish experience in Virginia is not unusual. As with other groups who have come here, Virginia's Jews have found a home.

NOTE ON SOURCES

THE stories told, and the materials on display in the exhibition, have been gathered from numerous sources. The American Jewish Historical Society in Waltham, Massachusetts, and the American Jewish Archives in Cincinnati are national repositories of materials relating to the Jewish experience on a national scale. In Virginia, the Beth Ahabah Museum and Archives is a treasure trove not just for Richmond but for many other parts of the commonwealth as well. The Ohef Sholom archives in Norfolk, the Beth El archives in Alexandria, and the Rodef Shalom archives in Falls Church also have important sources.

In terms of printed materials, a number of articles have been published in *American Jewish History* and its predecessor volumes dating back to the turn of the century, as well as in *American Jewish Archives*, the *Virginia Magazine of History and Biography*, and local history journals. Readers interested in secondary literature are referred to the following works:

Berman, Myron. *Richmond's Jewry, 1769–1976: Shabbat in Shockoe*. Charlottesville, 1979.

Cohen, Naomi W. *Jews in Christian America: The Pursuit of Religious Equality*. New York, 1992.

Dinnerstein, Leonard, and Mary Dale Palsson, eds. *Jews in the South*. Baton Rouge, 1973.

Ely, Carol, Jeffrey Hantman, and Phyllis Leffler. *To Seek the Peace of the City: Jewish Life in Charlottesville*. Charlottesville, 1994.

Evans, Eli N. *The Provincials: A Personal History of the Jews in the South*. New York, 1973.

Ezekiel, Herbert T., and Gaston Lichtenstein. *The History of the Jews of Richmond from 1769 to 1917*. Richmond, 1917.

Feingold, Henry, ed. *The Jewish People in America*. 5 vols. Baltimore, 1992.

Ginsberg, Louis. *Chapters on the Jews of Virginia, 1658–1900*. Petersburg, 1969.

——————. *History of the Jews of Petersburg, 1789–1950*. Petersburg, 1954.

Korn, Bertram Wallace. *American Jewry and the Civil War*. Philadelphia, 1951.

Marcus, Jacob Rader. *Early American Jewry*. 2 vols. Philadelphia, 1951–53.

Margolius, Elise Levy. *One Hundred and Twenty-Fifth Anniversary, Ohef Sholom Temple, 1844–1969*. Norfolk, 1970.

Rosenberg, Max, and Arthur Marmor. *Temple Beth El: A Centennial History of Beth El Hebrew Congregation*. Alexandria, 1962.

Valentine Museum. *Free to Profess: The First Century of Richmond Jewry, 1786–1886*. Richmond, [1986].

Virginia-Israel Commission. *Report to Governor Gerald L. Baliles*. Richmond, 1988.

LIST OF BENEFACTORS

Bert Aaron
Dr. and Mrs. William M. Bangel
Mrs. Jay David Barr
Mr. and Mrs. Jacob Brown
Barry and Ellen Chernack
Edwin Cohen
Hon. Ezra and Katherine M. Cohen
Jeanne S. Cohen
Charles N. Cooper
Mr. and Mrs. Charles N. Cooper
Mr. and Mrs. E. D. David
Mr. and Mrs. Erwin B. Drucker
Mr. and Mrs. Daniel Dubansky
First Union National Bank of Virginia
Mr. and Mrs. Ralph M. Goldstein
Mr. and Mrs. Jerome Gordon
Jerome and Gigi Gumenick
Mr. and Mrs. Eric Heiner
Mr. and Mrs. Irving I. Held, Jr.
Mr. and Mrs. Lewis I. Held
Marsha F. Hurwitz
Jewish Community Federation of Richmond
Mr. and Mrs. Malcolm Kalman
Ettalea E. Kanter
George M. Kaufman
Mr. and Mrs. Philip W. Klaus
Edith Nachman Legum
Mr. and Mrs. Eugene M. Levin
Lynchburg Jewish Community Council
Markel Corporation
Mr. and Mrs. Michael Marsiglia
Mr. and Mrs. Milton Meyer, Jr.
Mr. and Mrs. S. Sidney Meyers
David E. Morewitz
Robert C. Nusbaum
Peninsula Jewish Historical Society